Sensible Leadersl

This book is part of the Human Centered Book Trilogy, the 2021 volumes of the Routledge Human Centered Management HCM Series. HCM books are pioneering transformation from the traditional humans as-a-resource approach of the industrial past, to the humans at the center management and organizational paradigm of the 21st century. HCM is built on the talent and wellbeing of people in the workplace driving work engagement, quality standards, high performance and productivity for long-term organizational sustainability in the global VUCA (volatile, uncertain, complex, ambiguous) environment.

This book was carefully crafted by recognized human centered scholars emphasizing the need for a new type of leader responsive to the challenges of the knowledge age, global connectivity and instant communications. The book displays a comprehensive framework for the transformation of common individuals into sensible leaders with high capacity to improve organizational culture using Soft Skills to meet critical responsibilities. Sensible leaders are human centered, insightful, prudent, focused on the needs and feelings of followers. They are integral and ethical leaders serving as guides, coaches and mentors, not forcing followers but perceiving clues and responding promptly to solve organizational challenges. They perform honorably in personal and work environments always caring for the common good.

This and its two complementary titles *Human Centered Organizational Culture: Global Dimensions* and *Soft Skills for Human Centered Management and Global Sustainability* are timely readings for leaders, managers, researchers, academics, practitioners, students and the general public working in organizations across industries and sectors worldwide pursuing quality standards, organizational transformation and sustainability.

Nicolas Majluf is Emeritus Professor in the School of Engineering at Pontificia Universidad Católica de Chile.

Nureya Abarca is Professor in the Business School at Pontificia Universidad Católica de Chile.

Human Centered Management Book Series

The purpose of the book series is to re-position people to be at the center of organizations, the economy and society. Using management as the common denominator, the ultimate goal is to perform a paradigm shift from the entrenched approaches of the industrial past to a human-centered methodology which is convergent with the needs of people and organizations in the constantly changing interconnected world that frames the new Knowledge Society.

The challenges that management is facing when dealing with human development, active participation, responsible leadership, financial accountability, and social responsibility issues can only be understood and solved through the cross-fertilization of ideas from different disciplines. Better integration between management, psychology, neuroscience, economics, education, business and others, needs to happen to accrue the benefits. The reason is simple. Global conditions create increasingly complex problems that can be highly disruptive. Solutions require approaches that build resilience through embedding multidisciplinary models that are effective in building productive organizations, transparent markets, sustainable economies and inclusive societies.

Maria-Teresa Lepeley, Peter Essens, Nicholas J. Beutell, Book Series Editors

Other Books in the Series

Human Centered Management
The 5 Pillars of Organizational Quality and Global Sustainability
Maria-Teresa Lepeley

Rethinking Leadership
A Human Centered Approach to Management Ethics
Roland Bardy

Wellbeing for Sustainability in the Global Workplace
Edited by Paola Ochoa, Maria-Teresa Lepeley, Peter Essens

Wellbeing of Women in Entrepreneurship
A Global Perspective
Edited by Maria-Teresa Lepeley, Katherina Kuschel, Nicholas j Beutell, Nicky Pouw, Emiel L Eijdenberg

For more information about this series, please visit:
www.routledge.com/Human-Centered-Management/book-series/HUMCM

Sensible Leadership

Human Centered, Insightful
and Prudent

Nicolas Majluf and Nureya Abarca

Routledge
Taylor & Francis Group

NEW YORK AND LONDON

First published 2021
by Routledge
605 Third Avenue, New York, NY 10158

and by Routledge
2 Park Square, Milton Park, Abingdon, Oxon OX14 4RN

Routledge is an imprint of the Taylor & Francis Group, an informa business

Library of Congress Cataloging-in-Publication Data
Names: Majluf, Nicolás S., 1945– author. | Abarca Melo, Nureya, author.
Title: Sensible leadership : human centered, insightful and
prudent / Nicolás Majluf and Nureya Abarca.
Description: New York, NY : Routledge, 2021. |
Series: Human centered management |
Includes bibliographical references and index.
Identifiers: LCCN 2020046799 (print) | LCCN 2020046800 (ebook) |
ISBN 9780367550721 (hbk) | ISBN 9781003091844 (ebk)
Subjects: LCSH: Leadership. | Management–Social aspects. |
Organizational behavior.
Classification: LCC HD57.7 .M344 2021 (print) |
LCC HD57.7 (ebook) | DDC 658.4/092–dc23
LC record available at https://lccn.loc.gov/2020046799
LC ebook record available at https://lccn.loc.gov/2020046800

ISBN: 978-0-367-55072-1 (hbk)
ISBN: 978-0-367-55074-5 (pbk)

Typeset in Sabon
by Newgen Publishing UK

To our beloved families

Contents

Acknowledgments

We thank the editors of this series, Maria Teresa Lepeley, Peter Essens and Nicholas Beutell, whose careful edition of our first writing has considerably improved this book.

Foreword by Arnoldo C. Hax

My good friends Nicolas Majluf and Nureya Abarca asked me to write the Foreword of the *Sensible Leadership* book, which is part of Routledge's Human Centered Management series. I was somewhat surprised by their request but delighted and excited to carry it out. Nicolas and I have collaborated in research for many years. I have been an academic at MIT Sloan since 1972. My main area of work has been Strategy, and before that, Operations Management. At first sight, both fields may seem far removed from the focus of this leadership book. But, if we look from the human centered management perspective, both subjects are, indeed, oriented at improving the well-being of people in 21st-century organizations. Only human talent has the potential to solve big problems in organizations and society.

All my research and last books on strategy are about the Delta Model. I created this model to call attention to the needs of customers. Without customers, organizations have no reason to exist. The key to success depends on the degree of bonding business firms can establish with them. Thus, the strategy focuses on one customer at a time. Sensible Leadership is a *sine qua non* condition to target a customer.

I'm going to comment on some of the themes and messages of the book from the perspective of the Delta Model and in close alignment with John C. Maxell's definition of leadership: *A leader is a person who knows the way, goes the way, and shows the way. A good leader has a futuristic vision and knows how to turn ideas into real actions and success stories in today's world.*

I briefly refer here to a few ideas or *Haxioms* (Hax's Axioms) that I use to summarize the lessons of the Delta Model, to highlight important and novel messages of management this book is conveying.

- The Delta Model focuses on the customer and their degree of bonding with the business firm. Similarly, this book on Sensible Leadership places human beings at the center of attention. Also, it emphasizes different forms of constructive and positive relationships among leaders and followers.
- The Delta Model stresses that you don't win by beating competitors; you win by generating a bond of mutual trust and affection with

the customer. When customers' relationships are well-balanced and transparent, the results are mutual benefits and long-term sustainability. This book highlights the critical importance of Sensible Leadership in the Knowledge Economy. In this age of instant world communications, effective leaders no longer succeed by imposing and coercing coworkers, neither using power as a mechanism of intimidation. Sensible Leadership is strengthened when based on a subtle influence and weakened with forceful behaviors.

- In the Delta Model, the strategy is not confrontation, but love. The strategy is not rivalry or focused on defeating competitors. On the contrary, a good strategy anchors in mutual understanding, collaboration, and, YES! Love! A word that seems foreign to this subject but is at the core of Human Centered Management and urgently needed in the times we are living. This book conveys this uniquely and graphically when discussing Emotional Intelligence, social talent, empathy in the workplace, effective communications, win-win negotiation and the ethical dimension of management.
- The Delta Model deals with the business firm in the context of its ecosystem of customers, suppliers and complementary businesses. All are members of a community serving the needs of customers. This book facilitates the understanding of the relevant contexts of sensible leaders. It is not enough to focus on the internal environment. The actions and decisions of leaders affect interpersonal relations, the political climate of organizations and society at large. In all situations, sensible leaders must be *human centered*, and act with *insight* and *prudence*. These are attributes inherent to effective leadership. This conception is a valuable contribution that trustworthy leaders in all industries, sectors and nations around the world should always remember.

Furthermore, the book provides contemporary executives with a useful checklist to assess challenges in issues related to the meaning of work, engagement, intrinsic motivation, work environment, empathy and many others.

The book closes with two compelling messages:

- *The sensible leader must be an "integral leader".* They cannot be leaders only in the workplace. They must be leaders everywhere, taking special care mainly in the wellbeing of their families and communities. They must also assume responsibility for their continuous self-improvement as a necessary condition for their personal development as human beings.
- *The sensible leader is an "ethical leader".* Leadership is the primary force that shapes world events. History has been written, for better or for worse, by the actions of political and organizational leaders. Leading modern organizations and societies follow the fundamental

principle that organizations are communities of *people serving people.* Ethical behavior today is crucial to foster sustainable societies.

Nicolas and Nureya have accomplished a remarkable task in this book, which is full of fresh and significant ideas that are of high relevance for the critical times we are living in.

Arnoldo C. Hax

Alfred P. Sloan Professor of Management Emeritus
Massachusetts Institute of Technology

Foreword by the Editors of the Human Centered Management Book Series

The book *Human Centered Management: 5 Pillars of Organizational Quality and Global Sustainability* (Lepeley, 2017) that launched Routledge's HCM Book Series in 2017 is a compendium of decades of experience validating conditions that determine the long-term sustainability of organizations in all industries and sectors present in the global VUCA (volatile, uncertain, complex, ambiguous) environment. Worldwide organizations that achieve standards of quality and excellence and become most competitive in terms of high performance, productivity and economic success, achieve these standards with systemic and systematic improvement, only possible because the people who work in and for these organizations demonstrate high levels of work engagement on a daily basis invariably driven by these organizations' efforts to secure the wellbeing of their people in the workplace.

Maria-Teresa Lepeley, a quality management researcher and practitioner, has had unique opportunity to observe these results first-hand as an examiner of the Baldrige National Quality Award of the United States, and advisor to NQAs Programs in Chile, Brazil, Peru, Colombia and Ecuador and related NQAs Programs in Europe. Lepeley's background in economics, management, education and entrepreneurship endorses the value of multidisciplinary approaches to find organizational solutions in complex environments in the 21st century. Her studies align with those of Human Centered Management scholars and authors of 15 of the 25 most influential management books of the 20th century recorded by the Academy of Management (Bedeian and Wren, 2001). Among them, W. Edwards Deming, Douglas McGregor, Abraham Maslow, Chris Argyris and Elton Mayo.

Lepeley's development of her Human Centered Management model consolidated when early in the 2010s she addressed the subject with Peter Essens. With a PhD in social sciences with extensive research on how people work, organize and collaborate to solve complex problems in organizations in diverse industries and sectors, including the military, Essens led key investigations in effectiveness within and between teams and organizations. Coming from different academic and international backgrounds, Lepeley and Essens found a strong common ground that high performing organizations in the global VUCA environment always position humans at the center: people are the engine.

Lepeley founded the Human Centered Management Book Series supported by the enthusiasm that a visionary Routledge editor, Rebecca Marsh, had on this emerging management field. In 2018, the Series added the book *Rethinking Leadership: A Human Centered Approach to Management Ethics*, by Roland Bardy. In 2019, *Wellbeing for Sustainability in the Global Workplace* was edited by Paola Ochoa, Maria-Teresa Lepeley and Peter Essens. In 2020, *The Wellbeing of Women in Entrepreneurship: A Global Perspective* was edited by Maria-Teresa Lepeley, Katherina Kuschel, Nicholas J. Beutell, Nicky Pouw and Emiel Eijdenberg.

As Book Series Editor Nicholas J. Beutell has made a major contribution to position the wellbeing of working people at the apex of Human Centered Management. A professor of management, business administration and health care management, former Dean of the Hagan/LaPenta School of Business at Iona College, Nicholas also has a background in quality management, and he developed the quality teams at Iona College leading to the AACSB accreditation. His areas of research include work-family issues affecting small business and entrepreneurship, entrepreneurial intentions and wellbeing with an extensive record of national and international publications.

Under the human centered editorial guidance of Maria-Teresa Lepeley, Peter Essens and Nicholas J. Beutell, the Routledge *Human Centered Management* Book Series has experienced substantial growth, which in a short period of time exceeded a hundred contributors, steering attention to human centered scholars around the world.

In this instance, the *Human Centered Trilogy* of books is enriching the Series with simultaneous publication of three complementary management subjects in leadership, organizational culture and Soft Skills. The books are titled *Sensible Leadership: Human Centered, Insightful and Prudent*, authored by Nicolas Majluf and Nureya Abarca; *Human Centered Organizational Culture: Global Dimensions*, edited by Maria-Teresa Lepeley, Oswaldo Morales, Peter Essens, Nicholas J. Beutell and Nicolas Majluf; and *Soft Skills for Human Centered Management and Global Sustainability*, edited by Maria-Teresa Lepeley, Nicholas J. Beutell, Nureya Abarca and Nicolas Majluf. This collection adds the talent and experiences of new editors and authors Majluf, Abarca and Morales to over a hundred HCM Book Series contributing scholars. All aiming for the continuous enrichment of wellbeing of Human Centered Management theorists, practitioners and readers worldwide.

MTL PE NJB

Preface by the Book Authors

We wanted to write a book about leadership. We had to define the content representing a new way of looking at this subject. It was not an easy task because there is abundant literature. But we were confident because we have gathered valuable material during many years of study and research on management, in the form of articles, books, class notes and others. Also, we wanted to take advantage of the information available on the internet (although it is not easy to separate the wheat from the chaff) and learn something new about management. Furthermore, we were clear about the perspective of the book. We wanted to look at management from the *subtle dimension*, which for both of us has a meaning that refers to the delicate core of the most essential and profound management issues.

The management world deals with a vast domain summarized in the word *context* with its many dimensions and meanings. It also deals with the very intimate: the inner world of a person, including motivation, the sense of work and life, and many other subjects defined to understand better what goes on in the inner world of people. Therefore, in any study of management, it is vital to choose a focus of attention. We decided to write about leadership.

We didn't want to repeat previous leadership models that are not enlightening today. We tried finding a new voice to talk about the challenge of being a leader in our times and give some insights into how to face this challenge. We finally made the first decision: to approach this issue focusing on the relationship between leaders and their followers. It is a minefield, because, like everything in management, the subject has a thousand different edges. For example, leaders can be managers or servants, or their leadership can be exercised by their power or because followers concede by accepting them as guides and mentors.

We consider in this book that *influence* is a central concept in the study of leadership. Leaders are not individuals who give orders and oblige their followers but invite and provide support to them instead. Leaders have a unique sensibility to perceive the environment as much as the heart and feelings of people and coworkers. They are individuals who exercise their leadership, putting the wellbeing of people at the center and seek the most considerate actions and proper behaviors to influence not by force but by example and empathy for pursuing the mission of the organization. In this book, influencing does not mean an invasion of privacy or coercive actions. In short, they are human centered leaders.

Sensible Leadership has to do with the distinctive sensibility that good human centered leaders must have to *sense* what is happening in their environment and learn about people and culture. It refers to *three radars*:

1. The *emotional radar*, allowing them to detect the mood and feelings of the person they are interacting with.
2. The *political radar*, allowing them to realize the implications that derive when balancing power and influence in which all leaders are inevitably involved.
3. The *social radar* – which is at the heart of leadership in today's times – allowing them to anticipate the impact that their decisions (or lack of) have on the wellbeing of stakeholders, different individuals and groups of people inside and outside the organization.

Sensible Leadership is, then, the *insight* to understand and decode the relational, political and social dimensions of the environment in which the leader operates. The *insightful leader* may be perceived as subtle, visionary, penetrating, lucid, intuitive, imaginative, all describing positive abilities to understand the organizational context and the situation leaders face correctly.

Sensible also implies a *prudent* and measured behavior, to act responsibly and reflexively, once leaders appreciate the characteristics of the environment and assess the complexity of the situation they confront.

Thus, we came out with the title: *Sensible Leadership: Human Centered, Insightful and Prudent*.

The book has three parts.

Part I: Towards a Sensible Leadership Model

We are living through a time in which there is a great disappointment with traditional leadership. In this situation, people are willing to bet on newcomers who don't necessarily have a proven track record but represent a profound alteration of the status quo. We have a great need for leaders that propose an inspiring project and address our deepest needs, enhancing the meaning of work and life. When we idealize unknown leaders, this becomes a trap, harboring excessive expectations about their skills and capacity, which will hardly be satisfied. Today, in these times of high aspirations, and such rapid and massive communication through social networks, there is an accelerated erosion of the appreciation for leadership in general, because people's expectations are increasingly hard to meet.

To shed some light on issues related to leaders' effectiveness, we revisited some traditional leadership models to answer the question, "what makes a leader effective?"

- Trait theory assumes that leaders' effectiveness depends on factors such as personality traits or charisma.
- Behavioral theory focuses on leaders' task orientation and concern for other people.
- Situational leadership theories are based on the premise that effectiveness depends on external factors and conditions. Therefore, for leaders to be effective, they need to show the capacity to understand the situation they are dealing with and the ability to select the most effective management tools to respond to the circumstances.

These three models provide a multidimensional framework of traditional leadership that certainly facilitates understanding of the challenges of being a leader. They help explain effectiveness, but none of them emphasizes that in modern 21st-century management, the main concern is the wellbeing of their followers. Effective leaders must be human centered.

Part II: Influence in Sensible Leadership

Effective leaders emphasize technical efficiency and economic performance, but they go beyond those objectives. Their main concern is the continuous improvement of the wellbeing of coworkers. Harsh attitudes such as pressure, threats or coercion are not valid approaches to get the commitment of followers. On the contrary, leaders extend followers an invitation to be part of their organizational mission, without resorting to intimidatory tactics. Influence is at the core of Sensible Leadership. In this way, leaders build a work environment where followers can flourish and find meaning in what they do, strengthening their commitment with the organization, anchored in genuine personal and collective motivation to advance the shared organizational mission.

The primary way leaders can affect the behavior of their followers is through their performance. They are role models even if they don't intend this to happen. Followers permanently observe and analyze with great attention their actions and decisions. In this book, the focus is on a selected group of managerial practices that leaders use to influence followers positively.

The first managerial practice is creating a trustworthy work environment. Interpersonal relationships are more effective and sustainable when based on trust, which acts as a *social lubricant*. Trust makes commitments reliable, even in the absence of formal agreements. When there is trust, *words count*. One's word is one's bond.

Inspiring motivation and engagement and making work meaningful come next. Although these very relevant management practices can be studied separately, we group them as a unit. When finding meaning at work, both motivation and engagement emerge as a natural consequence. Leaders who can successfully attract talented people to get involved in the organizational mission also get their engagement and motivation. Followers will be willing to make a superior effort, beyond a simple contractual relationship.

Then comes the management of power and political processes that are always present in organizational life. Sensible leaders handle these processes in a very delicate way. Power has multiple meanings in management, and it is a very potent way of influencing people's behavior and actions. But only *subtle power* is in harmony with Sensible Leadership.

One of the most visible forms of influence is through communication. The saying goes, there can be no leadership without communication. Leaders address followers using verbal and non-verbal messages to appeal to their heart and head, emotion and reason, rationality and affection. Communication, without a doubt, is a central piece when influencing the behavior, feelings and actions of followers.

Finally, one of the most relevant and critical opportunities for leaders to exert influence is managing all kinds of conflicts that unavoidably arise among people at all levels, inside and outside of any organization. Leaders need to demonstrate knowledge and ability to handle adverse circumstances effectively, using subtle approaches anchored in empathy and respect for other people. It is a necessary condition to prevent conflicting situations from escalating. Sensible leaders are skilled mediators, but they may also be arbitrators. They know how to reach reasonable and fair win-win agreements. They are also the guarantors of the right implementation of and compliance with those agreements among different parties.

Part III: The Sensible Leader

This model recognizes two essential capabilities and three settings in which sensible leaders work. The two capabilities are *insight* and *prudence*. Both are essential because leaders' responsibilities are demanding, and their actions have profound effects on the work engagement of coworkers and the lives of many people.

The three settings are the relationship with followers, the political forces at work in the organization and the social dimension of management. They refer to the individual, organizational and societal levels in which leaders act.

We define *insight* as the leaders' capabilities to perceive and understand the relational, political and social context in the organization, which are characterized in terms of *three radars* previously indicated:

1. Relationship with followers: sensible leaders assign a high priority to their relationship with people, particularly followers.
2. Political forces at work in the organization: sensible leaders cultivate their political sensibility and participate with delicacy in power relations.
3. Social context: sensible leaders recognize in advance the trends of the social context and fairly assess the implications of their actions and decisions, exercising leadership focused on meeting the needs of society.

Once leaders get a clear understanding of the situation, they act with *prudence*, which implies behaving with moderation and respect in the three settings indicated above:

1. Sensible leaders exhibit *Emotional Intelligence* in the relationship with followers.
2. Sensible leaders rely on *subtle power*, diligently managing political processes and negotiation processes in the organization.
3. Sensible leaders place people at the center of their attention and focus on the wellbeing of all stakeholders.

Also, sensible leaders aim to be integral persons. They show proper behavior based on insight, and prudence at the individual, organizational and social levels of their work and extend their good habits in all areas of their personal and community life.

Finally, sensible, human centered, insightful and prudent leaders are *ethical leaders*, who influence the behavior of followers by inspiring their enthusiastic commitment and active participation in the affairs of the organization. They must cultivate their moral reasoning and exercise *value-based leadership* in their relations with people, the management of power, and the connections with stakeholders, so as not to lose the ethical compass in a changing environment. They also exercise *service-oriented leadership*, seeking the highest possible good and mitigating any harmful effects on people in and out of the organization.

NM NA

About the Book Authors

 **Nicolas Majluf** Emeritus Professor of Engineering Management at the Catholic University in Chile (PUC). He holds an engineering degree from the Catholic University of Chile, an Msc in Operations Research from Stanford University and a PhD in Management at MIT Sloan. He was Deputy Dean of the School of Engineering and Academic Director at PUC. He is currently the Academic Director of online management courses *Clase Ejecutiva* in Chile. His academic career moved from Strategy and Finance to Organizational Behavior. He is author of four books and many papers on strategy with MIT Professor Arnoldo Hax, and co-author of a widely cited article on finance with MIT Professor Stewart Myers with over 25,000 citations in Google Scholar. He has written books on Human Centered Management and Business Ethics. He has been a visiting professor at MIT Sloan, the Anderson School of Management at UCLA and IESE in Barcelona. He has ample professional experience as a consultant and as board member in foundations and many large Chilean public corporations. He has received numerous awards and academic recognition for excellence in teaching and research.

Nureya Abarca Professor at the Business School, Pontificia Universidad Católica de Chile. She teaches graduate and executive courses in the MBA and the MA on Innovation Programs and collaborates with the MA on Industrial Engineering and MA on Human Relations. She has served in multiple management positions at Catholic University of Chile PUC, including Post Graduate Affairs Chair, Chair of the Department of Psychology and Director of the Center for Work-Life Balance. She holds a degree in Psychology from the University of Chile and Master's and PhD in Psychology from the University of California at San Diego. She has authored several scientific publications in national and international journals and several books in Spanish including *Emotional Intelligence and Leadership* (*Inteligencia Emocional en Liderazgo*) (2004), *The Leader as a Coach* (*El Líder como Coach*) (2010), *Intelligent Negotiation* (*Negociación Inteligente*) (2017) and *Effective Leadership* (*Liderazgo Efectivo*) (2019). Her areas of interest include Organizational Behavior, Leadership, Team Work, Emotional Intelligence, and Negotiation. She is an organizational consultant and national and international guest speaker in topics of Leadership, Negotiation, and Emotional Intelligence.

About the HCM Series Editors

 **Maria-Teresa Lepeley** President and founder of the *Global Institute for Quality Education*, a research think tank focused on quality-based solutions for human centered organizations integrating education excellence with high-performance workplaces in the Knowledge Economy. Economist, educator and entrepreneur. Quality Management specialist author, trainer, speaker and examiner of the US Baldrige National Quality Award and adviser to NQAs Programs in five countries in Latin America. She holds M.S. in Economics (economic development) and M.A. in Education (Higher Education Management and Leadership) from the University of Miami, US, B.S. in Education and English from the University of Santiago, Chile. She was Director and Professor of Executive Management Programs at the University of Connecticut, US and at the Department of Economics, School of Business and Economics, University of Chile, and President of Entrepreneurial College in Santiago, Chile. She is a Founder and Principal Editor of Routledge's *Human Centered Management* Book Series and Information Age Publishing Book Series Innovation in *Human Centered Sustainability*. Authored books: *Human Centered Management: 5 Pillars of Organizational Quality and Global Sustainability; EDUCONOMY. Unleashing Wellbeing and Human Centered Sustainability; EDUQUALITY. Human Centered Quality Management in Education. A Model for Deployment, Assessment and Sustainability, and Management and Quality in Education. A Model for Assessment.* She is co-editor of the HCM Routledge Series books *Wellbeing for Sustainability in the Workplace. A Global View and The Wellbeing of Women in Entrepreneurship* and Palgrave Macmillan book *Human Centered Management in Executive Education.* She is author and coauthor of numerous journal articles in quality management, economic development and entrepreneurship. She is an examiner of US Baldrige National Quality Award, an adviser to National Quality Award Programs in five Latin American countries.

Peter Essens is Director of the Center of Expertise of HRM and Organizational Behavior at the Faculty of Economics and Business, University of Groningen, The Netherlands. He received his PhD from the Radboud University of Nijmegen, The Netherlands. His research focus is on how people work, organize and collaborate to master complex problems in settings with multiple actors. He has over 25 years of experience in the functioning of people and organizations in diverse domains, including the military. Peter has been leading key investigations in effectiveness within and between teams' and organizations' interaction processes. His recent work has been published in leading journals including the *Journal of Occupational and Organizational Psychology*, *Journal of Management Studies*, *Journal of Organizational Behavior* and the *Academy of Management Journal*. He is an editor of the Routledge Human Centered Management Book Series and co-editor of the book *Wellbeing for Sustainability in the Global Workplace*.

Nicholas J. Beutell Professor of Management, Business Administration and Healthcare Management at Iona College, New Rochelle, NY, US. For a decade, he was Dean of the Hagan/LaPenta School of Business at Iona. He served as acting dean at Stillman School of Business, Seton Hall University. He developed a quality management team at Iona leading to the AACSB accreditation. He has been a consultant for Equitable Life Assurance Society, Public Service Electric and Gas and AT&T. He developed and ran a successful internet business for 17 years. His main areas of research include work-family issues affecting small business and entrepreneurship, entrepreneurial intentions and wellbeing. He is an active member of a research group on work-life issues among entrepreneurs. He is co-editor of a special issue on work-family issues in South Asia for the *South Asia Journal of Business Studies*. He is author of the book *Evaluating Scholarship and Research Impact* (Emerald) and co-editor of *The Wellbeing of Women in Entrepreneurship* (Routledge). He is a widely cited author; his publications have appeared in the *Academy of Management Review*, *Journal of Vocational Behavior*, *Journal of Small Business and Entrepreneurship* and the *Journal of Managerial Psychology*, among many others. He is a member of the Academy of Management, Eastern Academy of Management and Work Family Researchers Network.

Figures

Tables

Part I

Towards a Sensible Leadership Model

We live in the 2020s in a complex, global VUCA (volatile, uncertain, complex and ambiguous) environment that is particularly challenging for leaders. There is growing mistrust in leadership in many countries and worldwide in areas central to people's lives, such as business, politics and society. We are often dismayed with traditional leadership that is insensitive to the needs of people and communities. Nonetheless, we need leaders to guide us through perplexing times. These concerns have motivated us to write this book on leadership. The purpose is to provide a different perspective on a fundamental management subject because leadership quality affects most human beings' lives.

This first part of the book presents the development of the Sensible Leadership model. A sensible leader is human centered, insightful and prudent. This part includes three chapters. The first chapter emphasizes the need for a new and different leader to respond to current challenges and rapidly changing demands. It draws attention to the fact that despite growing evidence of disappointment in and with leaders, it is untimely and inappropriate to pretend that the solution is to discard leaders and ignore leadership. The second chapter delves into factors central to leaders' effectiveness. We start with a review of traditional leadership theories, highlighting implicit assumptions on leadership's effectiveness with the purpose of comparison. The third chapter is a preliminary presentation of the Sensible Leadership model grounded on three fundamental concepts: *influence*, *insight* and *prudence*. Also, the sensible leader is an *integral leader* and an *ethical leader*.

Influence is expanded in Part II of the book. The assumption is that leadership has significant effects on people's life and work, so it is fair to assert that there is no leadership without influence. The other two concepts, *insight* and *prudence*, are elaborated in Part III. *Insight* is the ability of the leader to perceive and tune in closely in the organizational environment. *Prudence* is acting with restraint and respect in all circumstances and with all people. Insight and prudence are crucial capabilities in three main areas of leadership: paying attention to the needs of followers and coworkers; effective management of power and political processes in the organization; and dealing optimally with the social context.

1   Leadership for the 21st Century

The study of leadership is a pressing need for the 21st century. The current level of disappointment and criticism of traditional leaders drives people to bet on new people, often based on image, disregarding previous experience. They offer to transform the current complex situations profoundly. The assumption is that taking the risk of leaping into the unknown is better than maintaining a status quo that is failing for too many people.

The Paradox of Leadership

Defining the appropriate leadership profile for these demanding times confronts us with a mystifying paradox. On the one hand, there is a deep sense of mistrust and even contempt for leaders. Simultaneously, there is a pressing need for new leadership to instill a sense of hope about the future of organizations and humanity, and to provide guidance, and show new ways to advance in the challenging global VUCA (volatile, uncertain, complex, ambiguous) environment.

When life becomes routine and unchallenging, and inadequate or unfair situations appear acceptable, good leaders question prevailing values and attitudes and the appropriateness of conventional behaviors. They try to move people out of their comfort zone, defying the status quo, and challenging personal projects. Good leaders also bring novelty to followers' lives, making them feel part of a collective project that opens opportunities to enhance human development.

Leaders' achievements may be disappointing, but people feel relieved when someone is able to capture their attention and gain their confidence. Although they may have uncertainty about their performance as leaders, they are willing to bet on them and trust them. Followers feel grateful for leaders who propose challenging and creative projects with the potential to enhance their lives and open opportunities for personal and professional growth. A good leader responds to the deepest needs of followers, such as security and wellbeing, and gives meaning to life and work, which are crucial sources of their inner motivation.

An inner need for the figure of exceptional leaders, so ingrained in human nature, also leads to the trap of idealizing them beyond expectations. A common conception of great leaders often presents them as gifted with superior talents, intellectually brilliant with superb social skills and impeccable moral behavior. These kinds of leaders are prized as visionary individuals able to inspire and energize followers, leading them to achieve seemingly impossible goals.

There are many *ideal leadership* models, but the point to emphasize here is that people commonly fall into the snare of thinking about leaders as superior beings on whom to deposit their illusions and trust.

An example of ideal leadership, known in the literature as the *Transformational Leader* discussed in detail in Chapter 5, shows that followers and team members trust, respect and feel admiration for leaders and appreciate the considerate and polite ways of their relationships. Leaders who listen to them carefully can provide development opportunities and stimulate them intellectually. Furthermore, their vision of the future attracts followers, and their contagious optimism and enthusiasm inspire them. They idealize their attributes and behaviors and appreciate *individualized consideration*, the *intellectual stimulation* and motivation to participate in organizational projects.

From Idealization to Disappointment

Leaders are necessary to set the pace and progress of organizations and societies. We need the figure of leaders, and we idealize them and dream about all the good things they can do. We develop great expectations about how they can transform and improve our lives, alleviate our hardships and offer opportunities otherwise unavailable. So, it is not surprising that we end up disappointed with leaders when expectations are related to aspirations and not to leaders' real abilities to respond to people's multiple needs.

As human beings, leaders have limitations and are often removed from idealizations people build around them. In reality, the most relevant leaders are quite different from this grandiose image of superhumans. They are instead, as all of us, imperfect men and women, who have doubts, and make great efforts to overcome their shortcomings.

Perhaps the low esteem for leaders today is a reflection of an explosive increase in people's expectations, pressing for a greater demand for perfection and excellence in leaders' behavior, where minor blemishes become disturbing faults. Leaders can hardly meet these high expectations, considering the tremendous impact of social networks disseminating detrimental *fake news* and biased interpretations of facts. Fake news profoundly affects leaders' image, casts doubt on their skills and integrity, and damages their reputation.

Because of poor leadership, trust in relevant institutions has decreased over time. For instance, Gallup surveys show that between 1972 and 2018, people who have a great deal or a fair amount of trust and confidence in the United States Government and the US mass media (newspapers, TV, radio) fell from around 70 to 40 percent. The same is true of other institutions of great importance in the country for society's wellbeing, such as the parliament and the judiciary.[1]

Leaderships are questionable around the world. In Latin America, confidence in government is around 20 percent. In Europe, perceptions differ, from the Netherlands at the top with 71 percent to Greece at the bottom with 13 percent (Pew Research Center, 2017). The distrust of leaders in business firms is also disturbing. Covey (2019) reports that only 49 percent of employees trust their senior management and 28 percent believe CEOs are credible sources of information.

These are demanding times that, as never before, discredit leaders in all fields, across the business sector and political environments. It is a highly challenging situation that negatively affects countries worldwide because effective governments and growing businesses are two critical pillars of national progress and development.

These challenging times for leaders uncover a bright side, stating loud and clear the imperative that the new leaders reach high standards of excellence in behavior, as a necessary condition to bring greater good to people and societies worldwide.

The High Demands of Leadership

Many models proposed in the literature describe the role of leaders. Most focus on relevant skills they must have to be effective. Yet these are magnified descriptions that can hardly be met by any human being. The literature is rich in *ideal leadership* models (Giles, 2016; Bornstein, 2017; Zaccaro, Kemp and Bader, 2004). The demands are daunting, as seen in Table 1.1. We have grouped the requirements of the *ideal leader* into five categories: (1) irreproachable morality, (2) trustworthy way of being, (3) competent and active person, (4) inspiring management style, and (5) well-connected person. Suffice it to say that poor perception of leaders' performance is understandable because hardly any human being can meet all these overblown assumptions.

Projecting characteristics of the ideal leader is hazardous thinking. Leaders are normal people with natural talents but with the same limitations and shortcomings of all human beings. Therefore, it is necessary to understand the traits of an ideal leader as an aspiration instead of a real description of individual characteristics. Sensible leaders have the humility to recognize their shortcomings and do their best to reach what is ideal.

Ancona, Malone, Orlikowski, and Senge (2007) and Ancona (2019) present a different framework to characterize leaders' skills in five core competencies they call: sensemaking, relating, visioning, inventing and building trust.

Table 1.1 The *Ideal Leader*: Main Skills of Leadership Identified in the Literature

Skills of the ideal leader	
Irreproachable morality High ethical standards guide behavior, and there is consistency between personal life and life in the organization	• Integrity, honesty, righteousness, probity (doing the right thing) • Sincerity, authenticity (transparency and truthfulness, without duplicity) • Equity, justice (acting with equanimity) • Prudence, moderation (showing measured and thoughtful behavior) • Humility (being respectful, without overpowering) • Perseverance, persistence, resilience, patience, stoicism (facing difficulties without giving up, no complaints, no negative feelings, and maintaining self-control of negative emotions)
Trustworthy way of being There are many ways to achieve this	• Empathic, friendly, outgoing, kind, respectful, generous • Coaching (helps others grow as human beings) • Open-minded (receptive to new ideas and ways of doing things, strives to learn; flexibility to change their opinions, adaptable) • Restraint in the use of power • Self-control

A competent and active person who makes a difference
Applies with energy and enthusiasm their competences, skills and abilities and does not fear change, but instead promotes it
	• Intellectual competence, analytical capacity, abstract thinking, expert knowledge, wisdom
	• Problem-identification and problem-solving skills
	• Negotiation and persuasion skills, conflict management
	• Orientation to innovation and change: original, intuitive, innovative, creative, does not imitate, willing to take risks
	• Intensity, energy, strength
	  • Passion, love for what they do, motivation, they put no limits on their effort
	  • Unsatisfied, restless (achievements don't stop them)
	  • Optimistic, they fearlessly believe in *making the impossible possible*
	  • Self-confidence, assertiveness, determination to make decisions, courage to change
	  • Goal-oriented

Inspiring management style Achieve results through good practices, aimed at generating enthusiasm and commitment of collaborators, and work effectiveness	• Generation of a *winning workplace environment* that promotes creativity and tolerates errors • Clear definition of a project, focused (doing a few critical things well) • Thorough communication of expectations, objectives, and goals. Complete assignment of tasks and responsibilities • Empowerment, autonomy and delegation leave room for people's creativity and definition of their work

Table 1.1 Cont.

Skills of the ideal leader	
	• Talent management, engagement of highly skilled people. Concern for the development of leaders for the next generation • Team building: the leader attributes achievements or failures to all involved • Promotes participation and recognizes the contribution of all people • Assumes responsibility for their actions, not assigning blame for a poorly done job • Frequent and open communication
Connected Ample personal network	• Extensive networks, both internal and external to the organization • Knows when to collaborate and when to compete

Sensemaking: *Deciphering the Organizational Context*

Competent leaders can understand and decipher what is going on in the workplace, perceiving trends and anticipating changes before they manifest. Thus, they can respond promptly, seizing opportunities and challenges that organizations unavoidably face. The quest is to create a *cartography* of the workplace's relevant features, avoiding stereotyped descriptions. With this purpose in mind, leaders open opportunities for participation using internal and external information sources. They also initiate experiments to increase understanding of the organizational context continuously.

Relating: *Establishing and Cultivating Relationships*

Influential leaders have a broad network of relations in and outside the organization. They nurture networks of people they trust who provide support for managing the organization. They are experts at finding answers to problems they face, consulting coworkers across the organization and using external networks with the awareness they do not know everything.

Influential leaders are good listeners and cultivate fruitful relationships aimed at building strong networks. They understand the arguments and proposals presented to them and grasp their rationale. They manage to maintain a proper balance between their convictions and accepting the opinions of other people. They are good at explaining their points of view and anticipate reactions to their proposals. In this way, they offer persuasive explanations for their ideas and positions.

Visioning: *Proposing a Vision*

Engaging leaders articulate a powerful and appealing vision that gives meaning to everyone's work in the organization. They extend a comprehensive invitation to participate in the creation of a challenging and attractive future.

Leaders strive to make proposals that inspire them first and then move the entire organization, searching for a shared vision and shared values. In this way, they transmit their enthusiasm and *infect* the whole organization, when expressing their visions in images, metaphors and stories that move coworkers to action and promote a genuine passion for a shared project.

Inventing: *The Audacity to Take Risks and Innovate*

Great leaders develop new and creative ways to make their vision a reality. The very idea of the organizational project is futile if it does not materialize. The best way to do something is not necessarily the traditional way. Questioning the status quo permanently and paying attention to detail is a must. Experimentation with new ways of doing things and organizing work is part of daily life.

A common practice to spark creativity is to shuffle established working groups to force them to generate new connections. But it is at the individual level where the action takes place. To get high engagement levels in shared initiatives, leaders need to feel proud of their achievements when developing new ways of doing things and overcoming obstacles.

The Core: *Building Trust*

Trustworthy leaders pay great attention to their actions because they convey the meaning of the organizational mission and reveal their intentions. Leaders who act with integrity do not just talk about how important honesty is but are credible to earn their followers' respect. They honor commitments, keep their word and define a meaningful organizational purpose for themselves and coworkers. Their focus is on doing what is right and building a better future for the organization to improve people's lives. Their aim is not only to achieve personal goals or advance their careers. Of course, personal progress is a consequence of dedicated actions. However, leaders who cheat and lie are rapidly caught and can no longer last when they are insensible to the organizational purpose and other people's wellbeing.

Action and Reflection Leadership

Another characteristic that illustrates leadership's demanding nature is the difference between *action leadership* and *reflection leadership*.

Leaders must be prepared to make decisions and act in diverse, adverse and challenging situations. Overall, they are responsible for steering the organization with a firm and steady hand in times of crisis. At the same time, they must do their best to create a resilient and agile workplace to foster competitiveness and to address environmental improvement.

Leaders must excel in their day-to-day work and simultaneously find time for reflection. It is not enough to be good at action; leaders must also be good at thinking. Just as it is not right that "the urgent displace the important", neither is it good to have "paralysis due to excessive analysis". When too much time is devoted to thinking, the time for action will always arrive too late, and the right opportunity is gone.

Although it is not easy to attain optimal balance, real leaders harmonize the two skills required to be superior in doing and reflecting. They know how to integrate teams and assign responsibilities to attend urgent matters and pressing needs and prepare the organization to deal with future challenges. Outcomes are difficult to forecast because they do not depend exclusively on the leaders' actions and decisions. They also rely on the performance of people who work in the organization and, most importantly, on factors that fall outside personal control. For instance, this situation occurs with price changes due to market fluctuations beyond any company manager's decisions and control.

Note

1 Gallup data from https://news.gallup.com/poll/5392/trust-government.aspx

References

Ancona, D. (2019). Credible Leaders Walk the Talk: An Updated Leadership Framework from MIT's Deborah Ancona. Retrieved: https://executive.mit.edu/blog/credible-leaders-walk-the-talk

Ancona, D., Malone, T.W, Orlikowski, W.J., and Senge, P.M. (2007). In praise of the incomplete leader. *Harvard Business Review*, February, 92–100.

Bornstein, A., and Bornstein, J. (2017). 22 qualities that make a great leader. Retrieved: https://es.scribd.com/article/327136659/22-Qualities-That-Make-A-Great-Leader

Covey, S. (2019). How the best leaders build trust. Retrieved: www.leadershipnow.com/CoveyOnTrust.html

Giles, S. (2016). The most important leadership competencies, according to leaders around the world. *Harvard Business Review*. March. Retrieved: www.researchgate.net/publication/323229010_The_Most_Important_Leadership_Competencies_According_to_Leaders_Around_the_World

Pew Research Center (2017). Few worldwide have a lot of trust in their government. Retrieved: www.pewglobal.org/2017/10/16/many-unhappy-with-current-political-system/pg_2017-10-16_global-democracy_1-03/

Zaccaro, S., Kemp, C., and Bader, P. (2004). Leader traits and attributes. In Antonakis, J., Cianciolo, A., and Sternberg, R. (Eds.). *The Nature of Leadership*. Thousand Oaks, CA: Sage Publications.

2　Effective Leadership

It would seem easy to recognize *effective leaders*. By the same token, it is fascinating telling *exemplary stories* and legends of individuals who have changed the destiny of a country or a large organization. But it is less obvious why people should admire those persons. These stories commonly highlight attractive personalities, brilliant intelligence, extraordinary achievements or nobleness of their objectives. But the assessment of leader effectiveness is a far more complex task.

In the first place, many diverse audiences are assessing the leader, including coworkers, company shareholders and the external community. These groups pursue different objectives, use diverse approaches to get opinions and do not rely on the same sources of information, so the judgment of leaders' performance may be different. For instance, a company's shareholders care about business growth, financial results, increases in the value of shares and other factors that are by and large observable. On the other hand, the assessment of coworkers is somewhat subjective, based on personal perceptions about workplace issues, the warmth of the relationship with the leader and personal advancement opportunities.

In evaluating leaders' effectiveness, objective and subjective assessment components are intertwined, resulting in difficulties deciding if leaders are qualified when perceptions differ and do not match all evidence. An objective measure of leaders' effectiveness compares their promises to do something with actual achievement. For instance, it is easy to observe if the CEO of a business firm achieved the promised growth and profitability in a single year. Similarly, it is easy to learn about the number of new jobs created by the government. On the other hand, the subjective measurement about meeting people's expectations is not directly observable. It needs specific methods to determine people's perceptions of well-being and prospects for future development.

The evaluation of a leader's effectiveness is hardly limited to simple observation of objective achievements. Although leaders might behave correctly and do their best, their behaviors may be disappointing if they fail to meet people's expectations, even when they achieve organizational goals. This situation is common when the expectations of different people's cohorts are too high and can hardly be satisfied. *Perceived effectiveness* does not always coincide with an objective evaluation of a leader's effectiveness (Judge, Piccolo, and Kosalka, 2009).

There are situations when constraints arise due to leaders' shortcomings, such as lack of knowledge, experience or competencies. Still, challenges stem mostly from institutional, organizational or political constraints that are hard to overcome. Indeed, leaders' successes and failures do not depend only on the efforts they make.

An organization's success – often taken as an indicator of effective leadership – is affected by situational factors that are not under the leader's control. While leaders are flattered by successes and blamed for failures, good performance results from the combined result of different events, entities and individuals acting simultaneously. For instance, in corporations, achievement of goals is influenced by competitors' actions, new regulations, new technologies, interest rates, currency fluctuations and many other factors.

In this scenario, it is difficult to discern and identify the direct effect of leadership. Hackman and Wageman (2007) state that perhaps it is appropriate to focus on situations where leaders make a difference, emphasizing the context rather than their attributes.

All the above indicates that evaluating leaders' effectiveness is a complex and debatable subject that admits different and sometimes contradictory answers. Implicit in the various leadership theories is the criterion used to recognize whether a leader is effective.

The three traditional approaches to leadership in this chapter provide a clear illustration of this point. The Trait Theory states that personal characteristics determine a leader's effectiveness. The Theory of Behavior indicates that the effectiveness of leaders is given by what they do. The different theories of Situational Leadership assert that the way leaders react to specific situations makes them effective. Success depends on managing situations effectively.

Trait Theory: Personal Qualities Determine Leaders' Effectiveness

Trait Theory was the basis of the earliest leadership studies focused on successful leaders' personal qualities. These assumptions are most popular, though not always most effective.

In Trait Theory, leadership refers to unique personal attributes of extraordinary individuals whose decisions can radically change events. The account of their life inspires admirable and heroic stories found regularly in management and history books.

The fundamental assumption is that a successful leader is a person with great intellectual capacity, remarkable knowledge, emotional skills, physical attractiveness and virtues attributed to superior beings with such a level of influence as to transform people's lives. It is a model of an *ideal leader* and sometimes referred to as a *person born to be a leader*.

If leadership is a general personality trait, it should be measurable with appropriate psychological tests that identify people who show a high level of this so-called leadership attribute. The first studies of leaders' personalities were refined in the first half of the 20th century (Stogdill, 1948), identifying relatively permanent qualities that can consistently and reliably distinguish individuals with leadership traits. This knowledge was used to set foundations for selecting, hiring, training and developing leaders for future assignments to high-level positions. A synthesis of these studies includes the leader's qualities of knowledge of human nature, rigor in the definition of tasks, solid moral habits, verbal fluency, timely decision-making and high interpersonal and management skills.

Traits refer to coherent sets of personal attributes encompassing a variety of qualities that give consistency to high individual performance. *Person* and *traits* shape an inseparable unity. Traits differentiate leaders from others unable to lead, based on how they act in different groups and organizational situations. But this is a partial view because a leader's behavior varies significantly depending on circumstances, so achievements are not necessarily related to personality traits.

Judge, Piccolo, and Kosalka (2009) showed that a leader's effectiveness does not depend exclusively on personal characteristics. A leader's performance may be positive or negative, independent of personality traits that may be adequate or inadequate for specific contexts. For instance, it is positive for the organization to have a conscious and self-confident leader to set high ethical standards and an agenda geared towards the organization's long-term interests. But the same leader, making overly optimistic assumptions and following a dangerous course of action, may be detrimental to the organization. Similarly, a dominant and narcissistic leader who manipulates share prices for personal benefits certainly damages the organization. But this same leader, when assuming responsibility for steering the organization out of a difficult situation, may enhance results and contribute to wellbeing.

Theory of Behavior: Leaders' Effectiveness Shows in What They Do

Theory of Behavior establishes that leaders' effectiveness is related to what they do, how they act and their impact on the teams they lead. According to this theory, leadership does not arise from innate characteristics and traits. It is the result of learnings, practices and training. Hence the saying: "leaders are not born, but are made".

There are many activities, tasks and roles included in the descriptive models of leaders' actions (Majluf, 2011). It is said, for instance, that

PEOPLE-ORIENTED (SCALE 1 LOW TO 9 HIGH)		1	2	3	4	5	6	7	8	9
	9	(1,9)								(9,9)
	8									
	7									
	6									
	5					(5,5)				
	4									
	3									
	2									
	1	(1,1)								(9,1)
		1	2	3	4	5	6	7	8	9
						TASK-ORIENTED (SCALE 1 LOW TO 9 HIGH)				

Figure 2.1 The Managerial Grid.

leaders use their time holding meetings and making decisions. But leaders' work cannot be reduced to a simplistic formula because successful leaders are continuously reinventing themselves and redefining their work. Therefore, all models have shortcomings to capture the complexity of a leader's responsibilities and actions.

However, a streamlined Behavioral Theory of Leadership became popular. The theory presents leaders' work in a summarized way using two dimensions: *task orientation* and *people orientation*. Depending on the degree of attention to each dimension (Blake and Mouton, 1964), this model proposes to classify leaders in the managerial grid shown in Figure 2.1.

Task-oriented leaders pay attention to the technical and formal aspects of work. Their main concern is to honor obligations with third parties expecting full commitment of followers. People-oriented leaders focus on the needs of their followers and the quality of interpersonal relationships. Therefore, leaders located in the (9,1) corner of Figure 2.1 are purely task-oriented and exercise authority to achieve their objectives. In contrast, leaders in (1,9) are purely relationship-oriented, promoting open communications, valuing group consensus and personalized support.

The leadership approach of an individual is a particular combination between these two extreme orientations in leadership. When the managerial grid became popular, the prevailing thinking was that an effective leader combines task and people orientations in optimal proportions because *tasks* and the *wellbeing of people* must be taken care of simultaneously. Ignoring the responsibility of completing a task is not realistic but neither is completing the job at the expense of people's wellbeing.

There is not enough evidence to support that a unique leadership style accommodates all situations successfully. This assumption is the foundation of Situational Leadership, which proposes that leaders' effectiveness depends on their ability to adapt their actions to prevailing conditions.

Situational Leadership Theory: Leader Effectiveness Depends on the Circumstances

The central tenet of Situational Leadership is that different situations require different types of leadership. Therefore *effective leaders* must have two fundamental abilities: capture and characterize the specific circumstances they face and select the most effective management tools to solve the prevailing situation.

This section includes two well-known examples of Situational Leadership. The first is the Hersey and Blanchard model (1982), which states that leaders adjust their behavior to their followers' maturity. The other is the Vroom and Jago model (1988), which asserts that leaders adapt their followers' degree of participation in decision-making to the circumstances. Both are one-dimensional models, meaning that they reduce the identification of *circumstances* to a single variable and exclude other context characteristics.

Hersey and Blanchard Model

Effective leaders adapt management style to match their followers' maturity. For instance, leading low skilled individuals is different from leading high skilled coworkers. While the former better adjust to more precise instructions, the latter need autonomy and ample space to innovate.

Hersey and Blanchard (1982) define *maturity* as the confluence of *capacity* (work maturity) and *willingness* (psychological maturity) for people to develop autonomous behavior. Capacity refers to the knowledge and skills leading to high performance at work (work competence). Willingness relates to motivation, commitment and engagement to do things right and assumes responsibility for personal actions.

The ideal situation is to have followers with *work maturity* and *psychological maturity* because they can assume tasks and responsibilities with low or no supervision. On the other hand, leaders of low skilled workers need to provide more precise directives and closer guidance. In the case of medium skill level workers, leaders may open greater participation and involvement opportunities to stimulate their work engagement.

The generic leadership styles of good leaders, depending on the degree of maturity of followers, are:

1. *Telling leader.* Style appropriate for employees with low maturity levels, limited autonomy and insufficient skills. This leadership style is directive and needs to provide significant help and tight supervision, clearly stating tasks and expectations about followers' work.
2. *Selling leader.* This style is appropriate for individuals with medium-low levels of maturity. The emphasis is on coaching followers and using persuasion to help them gain more capabilities and autonomy

to do their work. Leaders present their ideas and expectations, providing needed information and offering support to engage followers.
3. *Participating leader.* This style works best when followers have medium to high maturity level. Leaders give them more responsibility and greater participation in decision-making processes, welcoming followers as active team members. Leaders' support focuses on the emotional reinforcement of followers who bring high engagement and commitment to common efforts and shared projects.
4. *Delegating leader.* This leadership style is appropriate for high maturity followers who can work autonomously and assume responsibility for assignments and tasks entrusted to them.

The Vroom-Jago Model

Vroom and Jago (1988) propose that effective leaders identify the appropriate degree of followers' participation in decision-making in every circumstance, ranging from autocratic to total delegation. There are times when leaders must act in a very directive way (offering low or no participation) and others when they can completely delegate decisions to their followers (full participation). Therefore, leaders' style is neither directive nor participatory but rather depends on the circumstances they face.

Vroom and Jago recognized the right decisions because they are rational (reached at by informed and logical analysis of alternatives), efficient (adequate amount of time to decide) and widely accepted (the team commits with the result), anticipating a successful implementation.

There is no ideal approach to decision-making valid for all circumstances. For example, in crises, an autocratic leadership style may work better, given limited opportunity to seek consensus. On the other hand, when allocating parking privileges to five employees of equal rank, it may be better to delegate the decision to them.

The Vroom and Jago model recognizes five levels of participation:

- *Autocratic I decision*: Leaders make decisions alone and announce them to the group.
- *Autocratic II decision*: Leaders consult with each member individually, but they decide and inform the decision to the group.
- *Consultative I decision*: Leaders consult simultaneously with the whole group, make their choice and announce their decision.
- *Consultative II decision*: Leaders delegate the decision to the group acting as one more member and assuming the coordinator's role.
- *Group II decision*: Leaders fully delegate the decision to the group.

People have natural tendencies to be either more autocratic or more participative or somewhere in between. To identify leadership style they must take a standardized test with 30 renewable questions about real-life decisions. In each item, leaders taking the test are free to decide the degree of participation they give followers ranging from autocratic to total delegation.

Numerous leaders from various countries and the most diverse industries and sectors have taken the Vroom-Jago test, building an extensive database for over 20 years, making possible cross-country comparisons to study the evolution of leadership styles. Results show that situations shape leaders' behavior. For instance, in universities and government organizations, leaders are more participative, followed by business leaders and further behind military institutions. Moreover, results highlight the importance of the national culture. For instance, Japan offers considerably higher participation than Latin American countries.

Vroom and Jago's studies support the impact situations have on shaping leaders' styles. Although personal traits predispose leaders to display certain behaviors to no small extent, decision-making about optimal participation levels depends primarily on the situation they face.

References

Blake, R., and Mouton, J. (1964). *The Managerial Grid: The Key to Leadership Excellence*. Houston, TX: Gulf Publishing Company.

Hackman, J. R., and Wageman, R. (2007). Asking the right questions about leadership: discussion and conclusions. *American Psychologist*, 62(1), 43–47.

Hersey, P., and Blanchard, K. (1982). *Management of Organizational Behavior: Utilizing Human Resources*. Upper Saddle River, NJ: Prentice-Hall.

Judge, T., Piccolo, R., and Kosalka, T. (2009). The bright and dark sides of leader traits: a review and theoretical extension of the leader trait paradigm. *The Leadership Quarterly*, 20(6), 855–875.

Majluf, N. (2011). *Los desafíos de la gestión. De lo formal a lo sutil*. Santiago, Chile: El Mercurio-Aguilar.

Stogdill, R. M. (1948). Personal factors associated with leadership; a survey of the literature. *The Journal of Psychology: Interdisciplinary and Applied*, 25, 35–71. Retrieved: https://doi.org/10.1080/00223980.1948.9917362

Vroom, V., and Jago, A. (1988). *The New Leadership: Managing Participation in Organizations*. Englewood Cliffs, NJ: Prentice-Hall.

3 A Model of Sensible Leadership

Traditional leadership models identify relevant factors to explain effectiveness in different situations, including leaders' traits, behavior, orientation to people and tasks, and the specific context. All are relevant factors, but based on our experience, we propose in this book a Sensible Leadership model for leaders to have a significant impact on human beings' wellbeing, which is necessary to attain high performance and long-term sustainability. The model includes three central concepts: influence, insight and prudence, and it identifies as essential qualities of *sensible leaders* being *integral leaders* and *ethical leaders*.

Influence refers to the thoughtful way that leaders affect their followers' behavior and wellbeing. *Insight* and *prudence* are two essential personal attributes of human centered leaders. *Integral leadership* means that sensible leaders' behavior is consistent in all realms, including personal life and work contexts. And the action of *ethical leaders* is based on values and oriented to other human beings' service.

Insight and *prudence* are present in three critical areas of leadership: First, the attention to the needs of followers and all coworkers; second, the management of power and political processes in the organization; and third, the social challenges of management.

Influence

We are social beings, and as we run our lives, we interact and influence each other. Mutual influence in human relationships is the norm and is unavoidable. When two or more people relate, they interact in different forms affecting their beliefs, ways of thinking and behavior to a greater or lesser extent. For instance:

- People may change understanding on a subject – *after our conversation, the issue of global warming is clearer to me.*
- change their opinions – *I thought there was more political clout on the issue of global warming, but now I realize its scientific basis.*
- or behavior – *I will sign up as a volunteer at the Foundation that cares about global warming.*

All of us continually exercise some form of influence when we want someone else to think, behave or make decisions differently. In some cases, attempts to influence others will be direct, verbal and straightforward. But they can also be indirect and non-verbal. Our efforts to influence others in organizational life are embedded in a continuous *negotiation process* to attain specific results that can simultaneously satisfy personal or shared interests.

The key to Sensible Leadership is to be respectful of others' ideas and points of view and having a considerate influence over followers' behavior. Leadership always implies influencing other people. Further, there is no one single way to influence people that can work effectively in all situations because each situation is different. The main aim to keep in mind then is to encourage followers to get them interested and engaged in order to enhance their contribution, improve their participation, and consequently their wellbeing. Thus, they become enthusiastic and motivated by the leader's invitation and freely decide to actively participate, without undue pressure, threat or coercion. Their individual decisions are based on their own will because they like what they do and find meaning in the leaders' invitation.

Leaders infuse meaning to daily and collective work synchronizing organizational performance objectives with personal goals. In this way, people link their convictions and the value of their jobs. Leaders implement management and communication systems that facilitate work coordination and ensure consistency of personal with organizational objectives.

Sensible leaders enhance the meaning of work, securing environments that stimulate solidarity and transparency in social relationships. The quality of collaboration, connectivity, communication and teamwork are critical. Also, organizational actions must respond to the community's needs to genuinely represent shared purpose and values (Rousseau, 1993).

Finally, employees find deep meaning when working for an organization with a sense of long-term purpose and a mission embedded in collective values. That is why one of the leaders' central roles is to transform the organization into a sustainable institution, with an unmistakable identity that appeals to followers. They value being part of an enduring and sustainable organization that adapts and responds effectively to a changing and unpredictable environment.

Sensible leaders succeed in mobilizing followers by influence rather than authority, developing and inspiring commitment instead of demanding compliance, promoting participation and collaborative behavior, not by resorting to repressive means.

It is unethical to exercise influence by breaking or manipulating the person. Supervisors who use power to maneuver employees may get a rapid result but invariably destroy relationships. This approach to managing is counterproductive because people are better educated and informed and resist more formal authoritarian leadership style, mainly in knowledge-based organizations. Kotter (1985) argues about this issue, asserting:

> Trying to control others solely directing them and based on the power associated with a higher position simply will not work—first, because managers are always dependent on some people over whom they have no formal authority, and second because virtually no one in modern organizations will passively accept and completely obey a constant stream of orders from someone just because he or she is the boss.

Moreover, in modern organizations, where hierarchies are significantly flatter, and globalization is the norm, leaders manage largely by influence. When operating in various countries, with different cultures, beliefs, values and conventional rules regarding acceptable behavior on subjects like participation, cooperation and team building, leaders don't have any other option.

There are different ways to influence people's behavior based on reason, social relationships and emotions, as described below (Bacon, 2012).

- *Influence based on reason* uses different approaches. The most common is persuasion based on logical arguments. Expressing ideas in a convincing voice is another way of influencing people. Being recognized as an expert or authority in a subject has a powerful effect. And finally, defining implicit or explicit incentives commonly leads to desirable behavior.
- *Influence based on social relations* arises in socializing, just from being an open and friendly person, finding common ground and making other people feel good. Appealing to the breadth and strength of existing relationships is crucial to achieving agreements with close people. Also, involving people in a problem or solution or stimulating them through participation is a common form of affecting people's behavior. Finally, when there is no easy way to influence directly, building alliances may work well. For instance, using peer or group leverage to achieve cooperation or agreements may help to gain consent.
- *Influence based on emotions* works when appealing to values. It is an important approach to engage people to advance the organizational mission. Religious or spiritual leaders and politicians use it often. Moreover, being a role model is a must for a sensible leader whose main attribute is to lead by example.

Research findings show that persuasion based on logical arguments is frequently used and one of the most effective approaches to influence followers in Western cultures (Bacon, 2012). Nonetheless, it may not be the most effective strategy when leaders seek to engage followers. In this instance, it is more appropriate to appeal to shared values and personal relationships.

Another relevant form of emotional influence is to observe the leaders' behavior because they are role models that can generate commitment. And when their leverage is not enough, leaders resort to negotiating or making concessions to achieve cooperation or seek support to achieve collaboration from followers.

These ideas are at the core of this book, where leadership is a process of influencing by supporting the goals that people value and by strengthening their connection and affection to the working community to which they belong.

Sensible Leadership

Two key leaders' capabilities are *insight*, meaning to perceive their relational environment, and *prudence* to act discreetly and tactfully to face the complexity of their responsibilities effectively. Moreover, sensible leaders are integral persons who perform appropriately and consistently in personal and work environments and give thorough attention to the ethical impact of their actions and decisions on people's wellbeing.

Insight *to Perceive and Interpret the Environment*

Leaders need insight to fully understand the complexities of the organizational environment and assess the consequences of their actions and decisions. They need to develop a deep sensibility to appreciate people's expectations from the moment they are appointed. Leaders must be selective and careful with their words and actions because all their deeds are subject to interpretation. They are continually transmitting verbal and non-verbal messages. They must be aware of the signals they send to minimize unintended messages and maximize those they want to communicate. They must favor clear, simple, direct and consistent messages (Porter, Lorsch, and Nohria, 2004).

The insights of sensible leaders arise in three settings: interpersonal, organizational and societal. They have *three radars*. First, an *emotional radar* to perceive the subtleties and emotions of their followers. Also, a *political radar* to grasp competing objectives and political interests of various groups trying to impose their views on the organization. And finally, a *social radar* to anticipate environmental and culture changes (social, cultural, economic, technological and demographic) and adequately assess the ethical impact of their actions and decisions on all stakeholders. Mastering these three dimensions of their work is a prerequisite to fulfill their responsibility and align with the fundamental principles of Human Centered Management.

Prudence *in the Exercise of Leadership*

Sensible Leadership is measured, prudent, polite behavior; it is alert to decisions and circumstances, weighing effects on different groups. The term prudence comes from Aristotle and refers to the word *phronesis* that means *practical reasoning* or *practical wisdom*. Prudent individuals accomplish what they intend to do, being careful not to lose their temper or hurt others during challenging situations.

Prudence implies paying attention to the practical consequences of behavior, especially in the face of uncertainty that involves a cautious attitude towards risk and aspirations. It is characteristic of a prudent person to reflect before acting and remain calm in all circumstances. Often mistakes in decision-making dealing with people or forming an opinion derive from haste, emotional outburst, unstable mood, a mistaken perception of reality or lack of adequate information.

Lack of prudence, resulting from unreflective and impulsive decisions, has a high potential to harm people individually and collectively. Prudence makes people reflect on the effects that words and actions generate in others, considering positive and negative impacts and acting appropriately in all circumstances. Prudence is related to what colloquially is called *good judgment*, which involves deciding on desirable behavior considering short- and long-term effects.

Prudence also implies taking care of future consequences related to goal settings and long-term vision. The temporal aspect is important because the effects of actions have long-lasting aftermaths. For the same reason, prudence is contrary to short-term impulsive behavior that lacks vision, planning and self-control (Abarca, 2004).

Prudent behavior resorts to accepted rules of conduct applied in thoughtful and careful ways. Sensible leaders interpret rules according to circumstances and know when to be restrained when situations warrant it.

In this book, sensible leaders act prudently in the three settings previously identified: interpersonal, organizational and societal. Prudent leaders have the Emotional Intelligence necessary to respond appropriately to interpersonal relationships and effectively manage political forces and decision-making processes in the organization. And when they relate to society, they act ethically, taking care of people's wellbeing inside and outside the organization.

Integral Leadership

Sensible leaders integrate work and personal life. They act consistently regardless of where or with whom they are. They are fully aware that dissociating life between work and home is conflicting and harmful. They strive to be better human beings, supporting the family and actively addressing the needs of people in the organization and the external community.

Human beings reach consistency in their lives when they are always the same person. All their actions are directed at becoming better individuals while simultaneously strengthening their family, coworkers and addressing society's needs.

Ethical Leadership

More than ever, leadership in our time demands ethical guidance based on values and oriented to others' service. To avoid losing the moral compass in a changing environment, ethical leaders must cultivate their moral reasoning and exercise *value-based leadership* and *service-oriented leadership*.

Leaders are seen as role models whose behavior is imitated by followers. They must live the values they cherish. Otherwise, their weaknesses and errors are a cause of great pain in organizations. And with the emergence of sharp journalism and social networks that expand the news at high speed and without limitations, inadequate or questionable behavior profoundly impacts the entire organization. Instead of getting the support and enthusiasm of followers, it produces surprise, cools their interest and disengages them.

Sensible leaders, centered in people, who are insightful and prudent, behave as integral leaders at home and work, and act ethically in all realms are shaping human centered organizations in the 21st century.

References

Abarca, N. (2004). *Emotional intelligence in leadership (Inteligencia emocional en el liderazgo)*. Santiago, Chile: El Mercurio Aguilar.

Bacon, T. (2012). *Elements of Influence: The Art of Getting Others to Follow Your Lead*. New York, NY:.AMACOM.

Kotter, J. P. (1985). *Power and Influence: Beyond Formal Authority*. New York, NY: The Free Press.

Porter, M., Lorsch, J., and Nohria, N. (2004). Seven surprises for new CEOs. *Harvard Business Review*. October, 62–72.

Rousseau, J. J. (1993). *The Social Contract and Discourses*, translated by G. D. H. Cole. London: Everyman.

Part II

Influence in Sensible Leadership

Influence has many different interpretations. In this book, sensible leaders' influence over followers refers to the many instances and options they use to actively inspire and stimulate enthusiasm and commitment to participate in the organization's projects. There are many ways to reach people's hearts and brains, encouraging them to contribute to common goals. But negative influences produce undesirable results that may induce people to withdraw from or obstruct projects proposed by the leader.

The traditional way organizational heads exerted influence was through hierarchical and bureaucratic structures aligned with rigid strategies associated with formal management systems entrenched in Planning and Control, Compensation, and Information Systems. *Formal management* has induced people to act as a *calculated reaction* based on established relations between performance evaluation and rewards. Their motivation is extrinsic.

In contrast, Human Centered Management (HCM) is founded on a radically different way to lead organizations (Lepeley, 2017). It emphasizes a holistic approach to pursuing the wellbeing of all people in the workplace. Economic variables like income, money, financial compensations and perks are important; still, the primary source of people's daily motivation and inspiration in HCM is finding meaning in work. People expect to have a job that offers them opportunities for personal development and professional advancement, as pre-conditions to increase organizations' performance and productivity. Self-assessment and personal improvement are vastly more important than the external judgment of other people. In human centered environments, people achieve superior performance because they enjoy what they do and *feel good* experiencing personal wellbeing, not just for money. Their motivation is intrinsic.

The analysis and assessment of leaders' behavior are critical in Human Centered Management because they are *role models* that people watch attentively and imitate. The scrutiny of their actions and decisions is continuous. Matching expectations make them respected and admired leaders for followers. When they do not meet these expectations, they are considered untrustworthy and unreliable.

This part refers to different approaches that leaders use to influence their followers' behavior positively. The first one is to create a work environment based on trust to facilitate collaboration and teamwork. Trust is a key *social enhancer* and an effective substitute for spending less time and effort formalizing organizational commitments. In short, a personal promise has more value than bureaucratic regulations. Trust is the subject of Chapter 4.

The next role of leaders' influence, developed in Chapter 5, is strengthening the meaning of work to promote intrinsic motivation and engagement. A good indicator of effective leadership is the *net flow of talent*. It measures the leader's ability to recruit, maintain and develop a sustained talent flow. As a result, leaders attract people with different skills who are willing to do their best for organizational success and sustainability. They feel the corporate mission as their own. They are genuinely motivated and ready to make any effort, even beyond the scope of their position requirements, to achieve the objectives. When people find meaning and understand the purpose of their work, motivation and engagement emerge naturally. They then show genuine enthusiasm for the organizational objectives and goals and the social benefits it brings to them and society.

Sensible leaders increase positive influence using *power* constructively and managing *political processes* as explained in Chapter 6. Management of power and political processes are commonplace in organizations. Leaders use both to promote their views, ideas and beliefs delicately, even among audiences that may be hostile to their proposals. But not all forms of exerting power are consistent with positive influences. Coercive authority and intimidation fall outside the limits of leadership in a Human Centered Management pursuing wellbeing in the workplace (Lepeley, 2017). Only *subtle power* is in harmony with human centered organizations.

Communication, another critical Soft Skill presented in Chapter 7, is used by leaders to influence people positively. It is the most direct and one of the most frequently utilized personal skills to affect other people. Communication can be verbal and non-verbal. Through numbers and symbols, leaders appeal in a compelling way to the mind and heart of followers. Scientific reasoning and artistic representations are effective ways to communicate that involve thinking and feelings. Communication is so crucial that there cannot be leadership nor Human Centered Management when effective communication is missing.

A final aspect related to influence, discussed in Chapter 8, deals with recurrent, natural and expected workplace conflicts, which are inevitable in human interactions. Conflict and negotiation are two elements that determine the outcome of effective leadership. The true temper of people is revealed in moments of high stress and tension. Reliable leaders are mediators and arbitrators of processes that all parties can trust. They can influence others calmly and respectfully. Also, they know how to lay out the basis of a good negotiation aimed at reaching reasonable and fair agreements (Fisher, Ury, and Patton, 2011). Simultaneously, they are guarantors of correct implementation and honoring of final agreements by all parties involved.

References

Fisher, R., Ury, W., and Patton, B (2011). *Getting to Yes: Negotiating Agreement Without Giving In*, 3rd Ed. New York, NY: Penguin Books.
Lepeley, M.T. (2017). *Human Centered Management. The 5 Pillars of Organizational Quality and Global Sustainability*. Routledge.

4 Trust
The Heart of the Leader-Followers Relationship

This chapter deals with the many issues and opportunities necessary for leaders to create a culture of trust in organizations. Trust is a fundamental dimension of progress, high performance and long-term sustainability. Trust is at the core of effective leadership and the focus of all the books in the Routledge Human Centered Management Series. Trust is not a given. It must be nurtured because when trust is lost, leadership can suffer irreparable losses. Leaders may exert their influence but will no longer get the affection or respect of followers. On the contrary, when followers have a great deal of trust in leaders, they can understand and even justify leaders' occasional oversights or failures.

Creating a Work Environment Based on Trust

Leaders who work hard to build a constructive and engaging work environment are trustworthy individuals that get the admiration and esteem of followers and enjoy recognition and a well-earned reputation. A critical competence of leaders today is to build strong relationships based on trust throughout the organization. Leaders thrive when they have the knowledge and skills required to build confidence across all organizational dimensions and promptly try to restore it when there are lapses. Bennis says: "Leadership without mutual trust is a contradiction in terms."[1]

Trust in leaders arises because of two main personal attributes. One is integrity, motivation and good intentions, and the other, achievements, professional competencies, knowledge and skills. Both attributes are essential. It is imperative to be sincere and honest, and it is vital to obtain good results. Outstanding achievements are not enough to build trust if the leader is a deceitful person.

The effects of the behavior of leaders on followers happen in many ways. Covey (2019) emphasizes the following:

1. Communicating with transparency and truth but being careful to avoid hurting people.
2. Being a good listener and showing consideration and respect for other people.

3. Being loyal and meeting commitments.
4. Making clear what the organization offers to followers and what it expects in return.
5. Getting good results and being willing to assume responsibilities.
6. Fairly evaluating positive and negative impacts of decisions when discerning the best course of action. And when someone must bear a cost, taking steps to mitigate the adverse effects of decisions.
7. Creating across the organization a culture of trust, emphasizing its importance in personal and collective wellbeing.

The Pillars of Trust

Trust may result from rational analysis, affective relationships and moral judgment about people's values.

From a rational perspective, people trust each other based on competencies, consistency and similarity. *Competencies* refer to knowledge, experience, skills and abilities to face and solve unexpected problems, or just to reputation. *Consistency* is about keeping commitments and showing congruency between promises and actions. *Similarity* refers to the commonality of interests, preferences, education and cultural level.

Affective trust arises from relationships based on fairness, open communications and a genuine concern for people's wellbeing, protection and care, leaving aside egotistic motives or opportunistic behavior. Affective trust emerges from enduring bonds of friendship and mutual rapport.

Trust based on values rests on a positive evaluation of a person's principles, social rules, ethical conventions and moral or community codes, such as integrity, transparency and loyalty. There are essential differences between rational and affective trust. *Rational trust* results from judgment about a person's trustworthiness, based on competencies, consistency and similarity of another person. There is a separate assessment of each one of these factors from various sources of information. These elements do not mingle in a person's mind. For instance, competence cannot be confused with consistency or similarity. However, when *emotional trust* prevails, benevolence, fairness and openness blend in a person's mind, implying that trust is a general and holistic appreciation of the other person. Thus, when a person is benevolent, this behavior means fairness and openness. The person is trusted because affection is overriding.

Asymmetry in the Leader–Follower Relationship

As previously indicated, trust has multiple dimensions and expressions noticeable in relationships between leaders and followers. Leaders trust followers when they have favorable opinions of their competencies, consistent behavior and responsibility to fulfill commitments. On the other hand, followers rely on leaders when they consider them fair-minded, open and showing concern about their wellbeing.

In the first case, the rational evaluation leaders have about followers prevails. In the second, the followers' affection for their leaders is essential, and emotions are at the core of trust. But in both cases, integrity and the consistency of values are quite important. Therefore, if followers want their leaders to trust them, they need to pay preferential attention to completing tasks and responsibilities, ensuring they fulfill duties, show competencies and maintain a positive attitude towards work and the organization. On the other hand, if leaders want to gain followers' trust, they must enhance the value of personal relationships, keep frequent interactions and maintain open and fluid communications.

The Value of Trust

Our early research on trust (Abarca, Majluf, and Mingo, 2003) identified the benefits of trust in organizations. In the case of a business firm, trust increases the firm's equity, raising its *social capital*. If a trustworthy organizational climate prevails, it significantly decreases legal documents, rules and written norms because *the word counts*. When trust reigns, people's promises and actions are reliable.

Trust acts as an organizational bond boosting cohesion in the workplace. It also acts as an organizational boost reducing friction and consolidating relationships. Covey (2019) explains this point lucidly, saying that "when trust is low, a hidden tax is charged in each transaction, each communication, each interaction, and each strategy", reducing speed and increasing the costs of decision-making. When trust is high, transaction costs decrease, productivity and efficiency increase and prevailing conditions promote innovation and creativity.

Yet all these benefits result from something more profound related to people and the way they interact. Trust and affection are interconnected. When a person trusts another, they acknowledge mutual appreciation. When trust is missing, barriers make the relationship difficult. The values and charismas the other person brings to the relationship are blurred. Trust is essential to develop strong relationships anywhere and particularly at work. Openness induces trust and allows people to realize unique talents that strengthen relationships, adding value to the collective effort. Social relations become more fulfilling, robust and stable, contributing to improving the workplace and reducing employee turnover. Even if leaders are harsh in relationships with employees, trust prevails, and followers do not consider their behavior capricious or unfair because they trust them.

Trust positively impacts the workplace, fostering people's wellbeing, the organization's development potential and profitability in business firms. Trust lowers costs of coordination, increasing participation because all information is openly shared. People get and enjoy more autonomy leading to improved decision-making, positively impacting results. Trust is critical to developing high performing work teams and outstanding performance. Committed collaborative groups of people are the most important strategic asset in all organizations, particularly business firms. Teams are at the core of competitive advantages. Building trust in organizations takes time and effort, but it is essential to attain long-term sustainability to face unavoidable disruptions in the global VUCA (volatile, uncertain, complex, ambiguous) environment.

Trust is an essential organizational feature today when people and employees doubt the organization's benevolence, which is subject to frequent changes that create anxiety and affect trust in the workplace. For instance, as mergers and acquisitions and *restructuring* are commonplace in volatile environments, organizations in all sectors and industries can hardly guarantee job stability, regular wages increases or substantial pension plans. The reasons may be understandable, but disruptions discourage employees and erode trust.

Rapid and constant organizational changes hurt trust. The same happens with diversity, autonomy and multiple preferences in the workforce. They can negatively affect employees' perceptions because expectations are numerous and varied, and organizations cannot satisfy them all, generating frustration and mistrust among people.

Trust has significant benefits for people and organizations, and its deterioration leading to mistrust has high costs and strong effects. Low levels of trust create barriers to communication that obstruct information sharing. People in the organization get suspicious even of objective evidence, hindering teamwork and harming decision-making processes. People become detached from shared goals and focus on their benefits at the expense of collective wellbeing, organizational mission and long-term sustainability.

How to Build Trust

Zak (2017) reports that people in high trust organizations show 74 percent less stress, 106 percent more energy at work, 50 percent more productivity, 13 percent fewer sick days, 76 percent higher engagement, 29 percent more satisfaction with their lives and 40 percent less burnout, compared with low trust organizations. Covey (2019) identifies "Four Cores of Credibility: Integrity, Intent, Capabilities, and Results". Our studies show that leaders able to build high levels of trust create a culture of excellence, offer more autonomy that increases employees' participation and show a warm and integral behavior displayed in the following activities:

Culture of excellence:

- *Set challenging objectives.* Defined objectives must be attainable subject to clear goals; otherwise, they generate frustration and people fail to get engaged. Leaders must remain alert and continuously evaluate progress across tasks and projects to ensure that goals are met and do not present hard to attain obstacles to avoid demoralization.

- *Excellence recognition.* Public recognition by leaders and peers for work well done is most valuable for boosting motivation when sincerely offered after goals are reached, and are individually granted and unexpected. It is an effective way to celebrate success and inspire other people who strive for excellence. It is also an opportunity to share experiences and learn from each other.
- *Facilitate personal growth.* Opportunities for professional growth at work, though very relevant, are not enough. They must be aligned with personal development that generates commitment, loyalty and trust, supporting work-life balance, leisure activities and the inclusion of other activities on the agenda.

Autonomy and participation:

- *Allow people to choose their work.* When employees can choose projects to work on, and attention focuses on their interests and concerns, competent people's loyalty and commitment increases in the organization. A stimulating environment brings out the best in employees.
- *Let people define how to do their work.* Autonomy brings greater satisfaction and promotes innovation as employees are free to explore different alternatives to solve their challenges. However, it is necessary to establish procedures to manage risk and learn from their own or others' successes and failures.
- *Share information widely.* People's engagement and commitment rise when they are well informed and future organizational development plans are openly shared. Uncertainty regarding the performance of the organization causes high levels of stress and negatively affects teamwork. Transparency is the best way to counteract most situations.

Behavior:

- *Build social relationships.* People that help each other and maintain healthy and positive social relationships create a respectful and trustful work environment that leads to higher productivity. Leaders who express interest and concern about team members' success and wellbeing are more effective, leading to a positive impact on the quality and quantity of work.
- *Show vulnerability.* Leaders are human beings and do not have to pose as smart individuals who know everything. On the contrary, they must show they need collaborators. This behavior is not a sign of weakness but strength. It generates trust and credibility in leaders and a natural impulse to cooperate among people.

Caring about Loss of Trust

Trust is hard to build and easy to lose, so it is necessary to monitor continuously. Leaders have the most significant responsibility for building and maintaining trust in organizations. So, they should be alert to avoid behaviors or decisions with the potential to erode trust. Among them, the following are relevant aspects to monitor (Galford and Drapeau, 2003):

- *Fairness and clear communication.* In Human Centered Organizations (HCO), all employees are treated equally under similar circumstances, and performance evaluations follow the same standards to secure high performance. Unfair decisions and ambiguous messages are banned. When employees encounter difficulties in doing their jobs, coworkers help them improve, sending positive messages to other employees. The interpretation is that everybody can learn from failures. In trustworthy workplaces, individual and collective best efforts prevail; indolence and laziness are out of place.

    An unexpected negative result may be the outcome of a business venture that did not turn out well. In those cases, supporting a person whose effort was unsuccessful can build trust. It sends the message that learning from failure is positive. It conveys that entrepreneurial errors may be acceptable when risk is a factor duly included in the decision.
- *Sharing information openly and widely.* Lack of information is a fertile ground for breeding apprehensions and rumors. This circumstance is mainly observed in problematic situations many people are aware of, and where information is consistently ignored or never discussed. Hiding information decreases trust in organizations.
- *Autonomy and delegating responsibilities.* Decentralization supports conscientiousness and independent decision-making of employees. Giving autonomy helps them define and control their work and become accountable for results. Organizations that thwart freedom and restrict employees' independence limit expectations, mainly among the most talented individuals who will feel constrained by lack of trust. Sensible leaders offer and expect trust from people, and this behavior molds the organizational culture.
- *Success breeds trust.* Organizational success helps to build trust, while sustained low performance hampers the credibility of leaders and organizations.

In sum, trust needs nurturing, but if for any reason it deteriorates, leaders must act rapidly to restore it. The first step is to understand what happened, unraveling the reasons behind the loss of trust, and identifying the people most affected. Then, make every possible effort to assess the magnitude of the problem and develop a solution to address the situation. Next, it is relevant to be transparent about what happened, explaining causes and impact on the organization, committing the best efforts to solve the problem. Ultimately it is important to make sure that everybody understands the proposed solution, explaining with transparency and candor about the estimated time to rebuilding trust and the efforts required from everyone in the organization. In the restoration of trust, leaders' behavior is vital in organizing the collective effort (Galford and Drapeau, 2003).

The Limits of Trust

Trust implies risk. It means taking chances on the behavior of others. A person trusts under the assumption that other people are responsible and able to keep and respect promises and commitments they freely make. But these assumptions may fail, and there are chances of losing. For instance, when a broken promise takes a person by surprise.

Although trust is essential in high-performing organizations, there may be obstacles. Trust is a principal component of a healthy organizational culture. Still, an excess of trust might be harmful to people when others take advantage, exhibiting mean or abusive behaviors. Therefore, it is necessary to maintain a constructive suspicion over time or a "prudent dose of paranoia", gathering information and observing people's actions and intentions to decrease the chances of negative surprises (Kramer, 2002). Prudent paranoia is a kind of Emotional Intelligence that helps perceive other people's aims that, at times, may not be as benevolent as expected.

Note

1 Cited by Covey (2019)

References

Abarca, N., Majluf, N., and Mingo, S. (2003). *La confianza en la empresa.* Santiago, Chile: Departamento de Ingeniería Industrial y de Sistemas, Pontificia Universidad Católica de Chile.

Covey, S. (2019). *How the Best Leaders Build Trust.* Retrieved from https://www.leadershipnow.com/CoveyOnTrust.html

Galford, R., and Drapeau, A. S. (2003). The enemies of trust. *Harvard Business Review*, February, 89–95.

Kramer, R. (2002). When paranoia makes sense. *Harvard Business Review*, July, 62–69.

Zak, P. J. (2017). The neuroscience of trust. *Harvard Business Review*, January–February, 84–90.

5 Meaning, Engagement and Motivation

A central responsibility of leadership is creating meaningful jobs that inspire and engage employees. Offering significant work is the most effective way leaders can secure their people's attention and wellbeing in the workplace. Giving orders or using authority to force people to do things against their will does not get expected or enthusiastic responses. Inviting followers to participate in a project they enjoy and give meaning to their work and life is the only way to get people to put all their energy beyond job obligations.

Work engagement is at the core of Human Centered Management. It is essential to attain quality standards and long-term sustainability based on continuous improvement of organizational performance, productivity and competitiveness in the global VUCA (volatile, uncertain, complex, ambiguous) environment (Lepeley, 2017; Ochoa, Lepeley, and Essens, 2018).

Work engagement is a crucial global concern. Gallup organization's *2017 State of the Global Workplace* reported that only 15 percent of employees in 155 countries feel engaged with their work and thriving, while 85 percent are struggling or suffering in their job.[1] Other European organizations also focus on people's wellbeing, work engagement and the impact of emotional, social and economic variables. Three among them are the European Foundation for the Improvement of Living and Working Conditions (EUROFOUND),[2] International Labour Organization (ILO)[3] and Centre d' études de l'emploi et du travail (CEET).[4]

Sensible leaders help followers advance to these noble purposes closely related to people's wellbeing and the common organizational good. Sensible leaders do not *act* or assume all responsibilities but *move everybody in the organization to act* and know how to stimulate and motivate followers. Leaders connect with people through their wellbeing, awaken their enthusiasm and get them engaged and voluntarily committed to advance the organization's mission.

Sensible leaders influence employees' behavior when they tune in with their needs, inspiring ordinary people to do extraordinary deeds. They create appealing work environments and shape organizational culture to stimulate people to do their best based on intrinsic rewards. They incentivize people to trust and believe in themselves, have faith and feel that obstacles are not as high as they may think. They go beyond setting challenging goals, and having high expectations, stimulating followers to pursue objectives beyond extrinsic financial rewards. Loyalty, passion for work and imagination come from the inner self of individuals. People value attractive jobs with a clear purpose and meaning that reinforces their engagement and motivation.

Meaning and Purpose at Work

Victor Frankl believed that "the greatest task for any person is to find meaning in their life". He asserted that "life is not primarily a quest for pleasure, as Freud believed, or a quest for power, as Alfred Adler taught, but a quest for meaning".

A statement of purpose provides meaning to an organization's work when it focuses on humane concerns employees understand and endorse, like society's wellbeing, environmental preservation and innovation that brings progress to humanity. Sustainable organizations consolidate these purposes in their long term vision. Therefore, a statement of purpose and values drives all actions and decisions of an organization. Employees must believe and trust it, strengthening collaboration in the workplace. This statement must be deeply felt and experienced by everybody, or it has the risk of becoming a deceptive and irrelevant document.

Proper implementation of the statement of purpose and values should be transparent in all actions of the organization. Corporate values supporting the mission statement should become part of daily life. Declaring that the organization cares for the environment and recycles waste is convincingly expressed through physical objects made of reused materials. Actions are the best way to communicate that values are lived and are not merely declarations.

Clear organizational purpose connects with employees' inner needs and aspirations, creating meaning in what they do and their lives. Finding meaning at work gives sense to life. It is not just a relationship among coworkers but also among human beings that integrate the individual and the collective to create a shared bond based on humanity.

Finding meaning is more important to people than any other dimension of work (Bailey and Madden, 2016; Maslow, 1954). Knowing the purpose of life and work is more relevant than money, career development opportunities or working conditions. The *purpose* is essential to move human beings beyond self and attain the highest human needs like altruism and spirituality.

Work and life are parts of the same human space. When organizations effectively integrate the work-life continuum (Beutell, Kuschel, and Lepeley, 2021), they attract, retain and motivate the talented people they need to build a sustainable future. It is the best way to design the type of workplace where human beings can flourish and prosper. In the end, everyone benefits, people and the organization.

The need to help other people and contribute to inclusiveness is a necessary component of meaningful work. It is essential for people, groups and society, not only for the individual. Abraham Maslow (1954) calls it a "need for transcendence", which he indicates is the highest in the Pyramid of Human Needs. This high-level need reveals an unavoidable ethical dimension to the management of organizations. Meaningful work implies becoming a better person that grows in intellectual capacity, scientific knowledge, artistic creations, professional proficiency and sports skills. But it also focuses on the benefits to others. It is not the focus on ourselves that makes us worthier, but the orientation towards serving others and the common good (Bailey and Madden, 2016).

Meaning in Human Interaction: Working For Others *and* With Others

Working for others is a source of transcendence and meaning. Having a positive impact on the life of other people is a source of significance in life. It occurs naturally in health care, where doctors and nurses assist patients to help them heal. The same happens in other profit and non-profit organizations. It is also gratifying to connect work and efforts with past and future generations, taking part in a long-lasting educational project or contributing to preserving the environment.

Working with others gives meaning to life. It happens in human centered work environments, where the atmosphere is challenging, and work relationships are polite and caring. These are places where hierarchies, positions, backgrounds, age or religion do not impede inclusiveness, success, prevailing loyalty, empathy, gentleness and friendship among peers.

Sensible leaders have a critical responsibility to deploy meaningful projects and create inclusive and considerate work environments. They can use different approaches to accomplish this. A relevant subject is time allocation for work and collegial activities where people have options to socialize and share experiences about their jobs, values and other personal matters. It creates a sense of belonging that allows for a higher appreciation of work's transcendence and its impact on people.

How to Care for Meaning

The foremost challenge for leaders is to ensure they offer followers a meaningful work. Meaningless jobs discourage people. Performance and productivity are impaired when people work exclusively for monetary compensation. The main problem is not excess work or long commuting time, but finding work trivial, worthless and futile. Inconsequential work aimed exclusively at satisfying basic needs is highly demotivating for the individual and harmful for organizational performance, productivity and long-term sustainability.

Bailey and Madden (2016) indicate that a careless leadership style is a destroyer of meaning at work. They present recommendations to avoid behaviors that induce people to think that their work is worthless. Sensible leaders give generous praise for a job well done and provide ample opportunities for developing individuals' creative, human and professional potential. Also, they pay attention to align their actions with organizational values to be reliable.

These five recommendations are intended to avoid common mistakes that destroy the meaning of work (Bailey and Madden, 2016):

1. *Promote congruent values among people, work teams and the organization.* The disconnection between people's values and those of employers or work teams destroys work meaning. This disconnection appears when the emphasis is on the *financial bottom line*, neglecting personal dreams and professional development opportunities. At the individual level, people's interests include quality and professionalism at work. At the societal level, it is contributing to improving the community and alleviating need. Ignoring these motivations impairs the connection between people's aims and organizational purposes.

2. *Be generous and truthful, giving recognition for a job well done.* Taking employees for granted is a significant destroyer of meaning at work. Recognition for a job well done and exceptional effort are a primary source of motivation. Organizations that fail to provide personal acknowledgment create a significant obstruction for workers to find meaning at work.

3. *Adjust work assignments to people's expectations and competencies.* Assigning people a job they consider irrelevant or unsatisfying is a destroyer of work meaning. People have a deep sense of what their job must include and how they should spend their time. They must perceive that their work is creative, compelling and inspiring and allows them to grow and reach their human potential.

   Employee's perceptions that the work they do is futile arise when they perform routine tasks, such as repetitive bureaucratic assignments or tedious corrections of previous work with an unclear purpose.

4. *Treat people fairly.* Unfair treatment of people is a destroyer of meaning at work. Sensible leaders take care of Distributive Justice and Procedural Justice. Distributive Justice means that people with similar merits receive equal compensation. Procedural Justice requires using the same criteria to address the organization's problems, measure issues with the same standards and offer the same opportunities.

5. *Open ample opportunities for participation.* Ignoring people's voices destroys meaning at work because of a lack of consideration for their opinions and experiences. The same happens when they must do a

job they think is inadequate, improper or marginal, or their views are discarded without explanation or deference.

Sensible leaders make sure people participate actively and enthusiastically. They pay attention and consider their opinions even if, in the end, they don't prevail.

Engagement and Commitment

Leaders approach people in various ways to increase engagement with the organizational culture and mission. Achieving commitment and work engagement results from appeals to reason (rational commitment), emotions (affective commitment) or a sense of duty (normative commitment).

- *Rational commitment* weighs the pros and cons of staying versus leaving the organization. The decision to stay compares monetary compensation and other rewards with alternative job options. It may also happen that an employee wants to depart the organization but does not find another job, so leaving the organization would imply a high risk of unemployment in terms of the opportunity cost.
- *Affective commitment* arises from the joy of being part of the organization. Work is a pleasant experience for the employee when they experience professional challenges and feelings of wellbeing. When affective commitment prevails, people feel engaged in their work.
- *Normative commitment* results from the sense of legal obligation and loyalty towards the work and the organization.

While an employee may simultaneously experience these three types of commitment, they do so in different degrees. For instance, when people are engaged, they remain in the organization because they want to do so. If rational commitment prevails, it is advantageous for the employee to stay in the organization. Finally, if the normative commitment is most relevant, employees remain in the organization because they think it is the right thing.

In this book, the emphasis is on engagement, seen in the pride felt for being part of the organization and remaining for an extended period. Employees identify with the organization and exhibit a deep sense of belonging and unwavering loyalty. Moreover, they consider goals and organizational values as their own, not as something imposed on them. Finally, they show great enthusiasm for participating in all activities and are willing to carry out a considerable effort to benefit the organization, being confident about their ability to make a significant contribution. Their enthusiasm goes beyond contractual relationships and shows in actions like volunteering, social work, support of nonprofit activities and other community and altruistic activities.

Motivation: Extrinsic and Intrinsic

Leaders gain their followers' allegiance by adopting two different but complementary approaches associated with extrinsic and intrinsic motivation.

On the one hand, they can offer salary, perk benefits, incentives and promotion prospects, leading people to rationalize and assess benefits and costs (*rational commitment*). On the other, they resort to a sense of duty and engagement with the organization's mission (*normative commitment* and *affective commitment*) that contribute to enhancing the meaning of work.

Good management navigates between these two forms of compensation: the monetary, to feed the body, and the non-monetary, to feed the soul. Leaders seek loyalty, generate enthusiasm, provide a vision and drive and induce employees to work hard. But to accomplish these object ives, often they employ financial rewards linked to productivity records and follow rigorous formal procedures for selection and promotion. This way of behaving relies on *extrinsic motivation* but may prevent reaching the inner drives of people's motivations.

Extrinsic Motivation

Motivation is extrinsic when triggered by a stimulus external to the individual. It may be a prize or a punishment (commonly referred to as the *carrot* and the *stick*). Extrinsic motivation compels people to perform a job in exchange for something desirable (money, power, recognition or other benefits) or to avoid something unpleasant that imposes a pain or a cost, like unemployment. Monetary compensation induces behavior. In these cases, people's initiative and engagement are not the focus of attention. Money alone doesn't buy the passion, enthusiasm and intelligence of people.

Yet motivation increases with financial rewards. Fulfilling financial and economic needs is an indispensable aspect of wellbeing and human survival. Satisfaction at work comes from monetary rewards and prospects of a job that allow people to advance personal growth. Both are relevant forms of extrinsic motivation but have limits. Eventually, after a certain income level, money is no longer significant as a motivating factor (Chamorro-Premuzic, 2013).

When people are moved mainly by extrinsic motivation and expect to receive monetary rewards in exchange for completing tasks, there is risk involved. Their performance may be lower than that of people who expect nothing in return. According to Kohn (1993), "Monetary payment is not a motivator." It may ensure temporary submission without producing a long-lasting change in terms of attitudes and behaviors. In a knowledge-intensive environment where specializations and higher intellectual sophistication are needed, individuals who work exclusively to pursue financial rewards are out of touch.

Rewards and punishments are not substantially different from each other, because in both cases, the behavior results from rudimentary forms of manipulation and operational conditioning. "Rewards are like punishment" and "deteriorate relations", because competition for awards or recognition has a high potential to obstruct cooperation among coworkers (Kohn, 1993). Also, relationships between supervisors and followers can collapse under the weight of monetary incentives, since employees may feel tempted to hide problems from their superiors to forge an image of success to show to those who control the incentives.

Also, "rewards discourage risk-taking" (Kohn, 1993) as those who work for the reward try to minimize the uncertainties associated with exploring new possibilities and, as a result, attempt to avoid facing unknown situations.

Finally, "rewards undermine interest" (Kohn, 1993). It means that no incentive can match the power of intrinsic motivation. When the job focuses only on what the person can earn, or the financial reward obtained, the conclusion is that the employee finds the work so unattractive that only a monetary payment can compensate it.

Intrinsic Motivation

Extrinsic and intrinsic motivations are inevitably present in relationships between leaders and followers. The approach of this leadership book is that intrinsic motivation is better than extrinsic motivation. But it is necessary to consider limitations. These may be due to circumstances of financially strapped people, a culture that overvalues material possessions, or company policies that privilege *hard finances* over *soft human relations*.

There are increasing shortcomings to organizations focused on maximizing efficiency at the expense of employees' motivation. Pérez López (1993) warns that "money is not a universal motivator" asserting that leaders should avoid persuading people to sacrifice other matters for money because this may turn against the company's best interests.

Compensation should go beyond monetary payment to avoid the trap of motivation exclusively based on financial rewards. For instance, a salesperson's variable compensation provides more money, and implicitly it carries recognition for a job well done.

Intrinsic motivation comes from people's needs, inner desires and passion for doing something because the experience is new and exciting, and they feel impassioned about it. Addressing the challenges of their job and succeeding makes people feel engaged. People need to achieve higher purposes to become motivated and committed to work and experience satisfaction with a job that "fills the soul, not only the pocket". Interest and enjoyment are of the essence for motivating work.

Therefore, in addition to extrinsic monetary compensation, people are driven by purpose, meaning and satisfaction. This sense of accomplishment in a task, achieving a goal or fulfilling a commitment is what happens when artisans take pride in their work, or an employee feels satisfaction for helping solve a customer's complaint.

Employees' performance, productivity and innovation increase when they enjoy what they do and feel their effort is worthy. When this happens, people are absorbed in their activities, diving into a "mental flow state" that captivates them to such extent as to lose the perception of time (Csikszentmihalyi, 1996). When this situation occurs, time seems to fly, and actions run non-stop one after another with no pause. That is precisely the moment when people fully display optimal skills and abilities. No matter how excessive, challenging or even unnatural this effort is, it means nothing to them since everything produces a superior satisfaction level.

A similar situation happens with other non-monetary rewards, such as congratulations from supervisors and the group recognition that lead to positive behaviors that salaries can hardly elicit. Psychological and emotional traits are crucial in Human Centered Organizations as sources of motivation and wellbeing (Ochoa, Lepeley, and Essens, 2018). That is why information and participation in decision-making are highly relevant for employees to feel included, needed and engaged.

In a work environment where job prospects and development opportunities are extensive, even a strenuous effort and long working hours seem not to exhaust the employees. Rewarding experiences make people say, "I love what I do, and I even get paid to do it". On the contrary, when development possibilities are marginal and working conditions precarious, employees express their feelings saying, "I should be paid much more for doing this". This situation may happen when there is no autonomy, employees face tasks they feel unprepared to perform, labor conditions are not adequate, and there are pending safety issues. In such cases, extrinsic motivation can compensate for people's work dissatisfaction. Monetary compensations are essential when people suffer from different needs or shortages or urgently need money. Also, when they feel unfairly rewarded or are looking for a new job. The rest of the time, intrinsic motivation keeps people lively and engaged.

Effectively managing intrinsic motivation is a decisive element of organizational culture in Human Centered Organizations and a key for employees' wellbeing and retention. Employees become engaged with work when they feel their efforts are meaningful for the organization and contribute to their holistic development. To advance this aim, people must recognize and understand the purpose of work and its consistency with beliefs and values. Human beings need to find meaning in life and work. Without it, people experience psychological emptiness, which can lead to anguish and insanity.[5]

Leadership and Productivity

The classical Hawthorne studies (Roethlisberger and Dickson, 1986) concluded that "caring" management and leadership that puts "people first" has a higher impact on productivity than other characteristics of job design. The wellbeing of people is a central concern. People matter the way they are, considering their strengths and weaknesses, skills, knowledge, professional background, aspirations and needs. The most effective leader is human centered, meaning supportive of employees, a good listener and caring about people's situations and constraints.

The Hawthorne studies also highlight the way coworkers relate to each other and with supervisors. For instance, if relationships between leaders and followers focus on altruistic or individualistic behaviors, are based on intimacy and trust, or are regulated by contractual agreements; or if the commitment is emotional and affective or formal and distant.

To a large extent, social abilities play a more relevant role over performance than hard-cognitive knowledge or physical ability. Employees value highly being part of groups with fellow workers. Their *need for belonging* makes them accept and promote group norms and social control systems. Thus, productivity results from workers' decisions and not from special supervision or superior work planning. Classical organizations, structured as a pyramid of control, focusing on tasks, close directions and conflict management, are not aligned with the foundations of Human Centered Organizations.

Concern for employees' wellbeing is essential for high work performance levels, organizational productivity and profits. But if this is the motivation behind leaders' behavior, it is a form of unethical manipulation. Intentions matter. If the intent is mutual respect to promote and safeguard human dignity, then leaders are doing the right thing. Productivity and profitability result from jobs well done. On the contrary, it is questionable if the intention stems exclusively from economic convenience. Since leaders' real purposes are hard to assess, it is also hard to properly judge their actions.

The Full Range Leadership Model: Different Forms of Influence

We use in our work on leadership and motivation (Abarca and Majluf, 2010; Acuña, 2004) the Full Range Leadership Model (Avolio and Bass, 1991; Bass, 1985; Bass and Avolio 1994). It recognizes three leadership styles, depending on how leaders motivate followers, namely:

- Transactional leadership, based on extrinsic motivation
- Transformational leadership, based on intrinsic motivation
- Laissez-faire, or lenient leadership

Transactional Leadership

Transactional leadership rests in a formal relationship, of economic and legal nature, based on clear objectives and quantifiable goals, accompanied by incentives and rewards that appeal to the collaborator's interest. It is an exchange relationship interpreted as "I give you in return for what you give me". The emphasis is on the financial relationship. These leaders emphasize clear objectives and goals and monitor work and assess performance. Their focus is on fulfilling work responsibilities to gain the employee's adherence through incentives and rewards that appeal to their interest.

Transactional leaders provide support to followers to fulfill their duties and achieve their work objectives, such as better results, more sales, a better quality of service, cost reductions and many others. Leaders consider previous performance and personal needs and characteristics, like self esteem, aspirations and preferences to achieve this end.

Once leaders have done their part, they expect that followers will do their best to achieve their own goals and those of the organization. For that, leaders use performance evaluations, *contingent rewards* related to the achievement of clearly established expectations and objectives, and *active exception management* when focusing their attention mainly on unexpected deviations of results.

Transactional leadership relies on extrinsic motivation, with well-defined goals and an explicit contract. The effort individuals make and their interest in a task depends on what they obtain in return.

Transformational Leadership

Transformational leadership lies in intrinsic motivation, not necessarily connected to specific and quantifiable rewards. What matters is the meaning of work, ideals pursued and moral values as inspiration. The contract is not explicit, but mostly implicit; it is not legal and monetary but of a psychological character.

Transformational leaders set high standards of conduct and appear to their followers as role models and trustworthy because of their attributes and faultless behavior. Their collaborators want to follow them because of the positive appreciation of their human characteristics, charisma, social skills, personal contacts and permanent willingness to deliver everything at work.

Transformational leaders act to fulfill their followers' expectations, putting their needs and interests above their own, thus getting their admiration and respect. Followers feel a deep sense of respect and admiration for them, beyond their organizational position.

Also, followers have a favorable perception of the way leaders treat them, providing *individual consideration, intellectual stimulation* and *proposing an inspiring organizational purpose.*

Transformational leaders treat their followers with consideration and respect and pay great attention to their needs, concerns and achievements. They offer them valuable opportunities for personal development, promoting their autonomy, creativity and intellectual potential. They act as a dedicated advisor, coach and guide and give followers broad responsibilities.

As a result, leaders get from followers a more significant and relevant contribution. They feel privileged for being part of an engaging endeavor. Leaders induce them to look beyond personal interests, making the organizational purpose, goals and objectives their own. Leaders also get followers to care for the entire group's collective wellbeing.

"Laissez-faire" *or Lenient Leadership*

In the Full Range Leadership Model, a *laissez-faire* style is a lenient approach to leadership. Leaders play an unassuming role except on special occasions, when results deviate from defined benchmarks in budgets and goals, or when a significant problem arises ("passive management by exception"). Or they never intervene, avoid their responsibilities, not expressing opinions on relevant matters, or providing support to coworkers, giving them ample freedom to do what they want (*laissez-faire*). They avoid setting clear expectations and defining goals for their coworkers and get away from well-defined agreements.

Performance and Self-Efficacy

People's inner world and their private lives dramatically affect work performance. Sometimes people cannot stop pondering personal concerns. For instance, people cannot avoid thinking about a sick child or a significant debt that must be paid when money is scarce, or mentally stay away from an obnoxious, bossy behavior. Conversely, how can people disguise the enjoyment of being part of a good project? Emotions are always present. They reveal feelings and perceptions, which emerge like a tide that moves people to act either with enthusiasm or with great effort to fulfill their duties.

Amabile and Kramer (2011, 2017) use perceptions, emotions and motivation to describe employees' inner worlds. Motivation is an essential component of this inner world that encourages creativity and high performance, enhancing engagement with the organization and strengthening the sense of belonging. But when motivation is low, it can transform work into torture, the organization becoming less relevant, and teamwork a burden.

Leaders who are conscious of this inner world try to do their best to boost followers' morale. Amabile and Kramer (2011, 2017) identify the two most effective leaders' behaviors to enhance performance in terms of creativity, productivity, engagement and sense of group:

facilitating achievement and recognizing generously and promptly a job well done.

Facilitating Achievement

Sensible leaders make efforts and consider all options available to help followers accomplish their duties because the feeling of pride and self-esteem from the successful completion of a task or the achievement of goals is one of the most relevant sources of satisfaction. This favorable situation benefits the organization that becomes more productive due to the employee's energy and passion.

Therefore, leaders' focus is to create the most appropriate conditions for people to progress. These leaders build an environment in which goals result from people's attitudes and willingness to participate in the mission. They are leaders who broadly share their vision with followers and are available to support them. Thus, their effort multiplies several times. It may sound paradoxical, but these leaders are *invisible leaders* who don't seem to be physically present and supervising every aspect of daily work. They are neither bossy nor pushy, but their absence leaves an emptiness that is hard to fill.

In a nutshell, leaders facilitate achievement by pursuing four actions:

- Support followers without interfering with their job.
- Create collaborative environments that stimulate relations among people, fostering a sense of belonging.
- Set clear goals, reasonable deadlines, avoid unnecessary pressures and assign necessary resources.
- State the importance of innovation, be open to new ideas, and reward creative work. They consider failure as opportunities for learning, and not as occasions for blaming people for errors.

Recognizing a Job Well Done

The recognition of a job well done demands managing sensibly and paying attention to followers' achievements to acknowledge and deliver compensation and incentives in generous and timely ways. Otherwise, it causes rejection and resentment. Working environments improve when people are recognized for a job well done. But lavishing praise when there is no significant effort or achievement is utterly counterproductive.

Self-Efficacy

Expectations of self-efficacy are powerful motivators and drivers of achievement. It is the foundation of emotional wellbeing and crucial sources of inspiration at work and a critical factor in high job performance (Bandura, 1997).

Employees who feel competent to undertake specific tasks assume a positive attitude to accept responsibilities and persevere when difficulties arise. There is no better reward than accomplishing expected results, and no more enjoyable moment than celebrating the successful completion of work. On the contrary, self-efficacy expectations drop when employees feel incompetent, uncomfortable and afraid to assume tasks they think they are unprepared to perform.

Perceptions of self-efficacy impact the course of a person's life when they feel inclined to accept or refuse to participate in events with significant potential to impact their future. For example, when feeling confident, a person may take challenges leading to work promotions or a meaningful turn of events in their professional career.

There are four sources of self-efficacy:

- The first is the positive appreciation of personal skills. Past successful experiences of completing difficult and demanding tasks strengthen perceptions of personal effectiveness to face challenges. Instead, solving marginal goals that require little effort does not produce the same sense of accomplishment and, in the case of stumbling, generate discouragement. Failing to achieve in a demanding, challenging context is a learning opportunity that strengthens personal skills and builds resilience. With special training, the negative impact of occasional failures does not reduce the perception of personal effectiveness and stimulates the "learning from failure" process.

  When employees acquire confidence in their self-efficacy, it is easier to extend positive appreciation to new and different situations because they firmly believe in their ability to perform successfully in many contexts.

- The second source of self-efficacy is watching coworkers' successful experience in difficult and challenging situations that awakes the expectation that "if others can do it, so can I". Although observing similar people is less effective than direct personal experience, it is also relevant as a learning experience. The essential issue is to choose an appropriate model, which may come from the individuals' environment or, in the present day, from the many examples found on the internet and social networks.

- The third source of strengthening self-efficacy perception is through a *mentor* who can modify the individual behavior via *controlled experiences* designed to underscore easy accomplishments and catastrophic failures. These experiences may just be *verbal persuasion*, a widely used behavior modification method that leads people to believe they can succeed in performing specific tasks inducing them to expect they can achieve their goals. Harboring optimistic expectations creates realities, but repeated threats and failures vanish them.

- Finally, in the perception of self-efficacy, personal emotional state and physical health situation are relevant. The emotional state is revealed in the degree of anxiety, fear and vulnerability to stress, critical when judging whether a person feels competent to perform a task adequately. Negative emotions decrease the ability to deploy competencies and maintain control of the situation. The opposite occurs with positive emotions. Also, individual health is crucial. Individuals cannot perform in the same way if they feel sick, are tired or did not get enough sleep. The effort to achieve results is much harder under these conditions. Hence, it is important to know how to relieve stress and get the energy to overcome emotional and physical health limitations. Otherwise, circumstances distort self-efficacy assessment.

Toxic Emotions

When people don't feel well in an organization, performance declines, wellbeing decreases and the workplace becomes a source of frustration instead of a stimulating experience. In this case, instead of asking "what moves us", the pertinent question is "what hurts us". Instead of being positive or pleasant, emotions become detrimental and "toxic" (Frost, 2003). Pain and grief are inherent parts of work and life.

Toxic emotions refer to actions and attitudes that negatively affect employees, producing pain, anguish, frustration and stress. It can lead to harmful personal behaviors (consumption of addictive substances, abandoning work) and detriment to the organization (reduced efficiency and productivity and negative impact on the working environment).

Frost (2003) presents the following causes that can trigger toxic emotions:

- *Incompetent, unpredictable, abusive, or unfriendly supervisors without social skills.* They exasperate employees with excessive monitoring and unnecessary attention to detail (*micromanagement*).
- *Malicious people.* Generate pain as a form of self-protection and lack of empathy, and are insensitive to other people's wellbeing and performance.
- *Acts of unfairness and mistrust.* Generate bitterness and pain by opportunistic individuals who break promises and misbehave.
- *Inadequate company policies.* Such as excessive demands, long working hours or unexpected changes in work schedules due to *company emergencies*, which unduly interfere with personal and family life.
- *Encouraging competition instead of collaboration among coworkers* weakens teamwork.
- *Showing inconsistencies between what is said and done* undermines morale.

To address negative feelings, companies rely on people displaying superior emotional abilities who can contain and help others overcome toxic emotions. Anyone in the organization can take this role, but leaders unavoidably have to deal with people's anxieties and pains and prevent negative feelings from becoming toxic. To accomplish these objectives, leaders need to be effective listeners, understand concerns, offer support when required and express interest to gain trust and motivate coworkers. People with these talents and charismas are a real organizational asset.

When having these positive collaborators inside the organization, leaders' work becomes more productive. They can prevent challenging situations from happening and avoid wasting time and effort in solving conflicts and employees' problems.

Sensible leaders create a considerate and caring organization, building a culture that promotes common values aligned with community concerns. They foster loyalty, responsibility and creativity and take special care in effectively managing stress. And when these organizations hire people, they give preferential attention to personal attributes and Soft Skills – mainly their ability to manage stress and conflicts – without focusing only on technical skills.

Notes

1 www.gallup.com/services/178517/state-global-workplace.aspx
2 https://ec.europa.eu/knowledge4policy/organisation/eurofound-european-foundation-improvement-living-working-conditions_en
3 www.ilo.org/global/lang-en/index.htm
4 http://ceet.cnam.fr/ceet/centre-d-etudes-de-l-emploi-et-du-travail-accueil-947519.kjsp
5 This is the basis of Albert Camus's existentialism.

References

Abarca, N., and Majluf, N. (2010). Liderazgo masculino versus femenino: sus estilos y sus efectos, *Harvard Business Review América Latina*, May, 74–75.
Acuña, D. (2004). *Estudio comparativo de la confianza y el liderazgo de hombres y mujeres*. Tesis para optar al Grado de Magíster en Ciencias de la Ingeniería, Pontificia Universidad Católica de Chile.
Amabile, T., and Kramer, S. (2011). The power of small wins. *Harvard Business Review*, May, 70–81.
Amabile, T., and Kramer, S. (2017). Inner work life: understanding the subtext of business performance. *Harvard Business Review*, May, 72–83.
Avolio, B. J., and Bass, B. (1991). *The Full Range of Leadership Development*. Binghamton, NY: Bass, Avolio & Associates.
Bailey, C., and Madden, A. (2016). What makes the work meaningful or meaningless. *MIT Sloan Management Review*, January, 53–61.
Bandura, A. (1997). *Self-Efficacy: The Exercise of Control*. New York, NY: W.H. Freeman.
Bass, B. (1985). *Leadership and Performance Beyond Expectations*. New York: Free Press.

Bass, B., and Avolio, B. (1994) *Improving Organizational Effectiveness through Transformational Leadership*. Thousand Oaks, CA: Sage.

Beutell, N., Kuschel, K., and Lepeley, M. T. (2021). The work-life continuum: the new Human Centered Organizational Culture. In Lepeley, M. T., Morales, O., Essens, P., Beutell, N., and Majluf, N., (eds.). *Human Centered Organizational Culture: Global Dimensions*. Routledge.

Chamorro-Premuzic, T. (2013). Does money really affect motivation? A review of the research. *Harvard Business Review*, April 13.

Csikszentmihalyi, M. (1996). *Creativity: Flow and the Psychology of Discovery and Invention*. New York, NY: Harper Perennial.

Frost, P. J. (2003). *Toxic Emotions at Work*. Boston, MA: Harvard Business School Press.

Kohn, A. (1993). Why incentive plans cannot work. *Harvard Business Review*, September–October, 54–61.

Lepeley, M. T. (2017). *Human Centered Management. The 5 Pillars of Organizational Quality and Global Sustainability*. Routledge.

Maslow, A. H. (1954). *Motivation and Personality*. Harpers.

Ochoa, P., Lepeley, M. T., and Essens, P. (2018). *Wellbeing for Sustainability in the Global Workplace*. Routledge.

Pérez López, J. A. (1993). *Fundamentos de la dirección de empresas*. Madrid: Rialp.

Roethlisberger, F., and Dickson, W. (1986). Management and the worker. *The Academy of Management Review*, 21(2), 296–320.

6 The Management of Power and Political Processes of Sensible Leaders

Sensible leaders know how to manage power to benefit coworkers and the organization. They understand the symbolic effects of their actions and decisions and know the implications of their words. Managing power implies establishing ceremonies and traditions that impact people and the organizational culture and paying attention to finding the best ways to address different situations. Sensible leaders rely on strategies and structure as tools to deploy effective communications. People with power shape their environment, and, conversely, the environment shapes people without some degree of power.

Power is a complex subject because differences between authority, leadership and degrees of influence are commonly blurred and misunderstood. This complexity highlights the need to clarify them.

Leaders have power over followers, yet not all forms of exercising power are consistent with Sensible Leadership, as presented in this book. Some sorts of power are opposite to a human centered Sensible Leadership. To develop this issue, we conceptualize the exercise of power using the *two levers of management*: *formal power* and *subtle power*.

Formal Power

The concept of *formal power* stems from a legal authority. It was introduced at the beginning of the 20th century by Max Weber (Weber, Henderson, and Talcott, 1947) and is associated with his bureaucratic model. According to this model, organizations define perfectly conceived and highly regulated activities. Tasks and roles are well-defined, decision processes are straightforward, recruitment and promotion of staff are based on technical and objective reasons, and employees' work is aligned with expectations of people higher in the bureaucratic hierarchy. The hierarchical organizational structure specifies roles, authorities and responsibilities that define power structure and scope.

Formal power allows leaders to define tasks, assign responsibilities and control performance. Individuals in positions of authority exercise power by their rank or status in the organization's hierarchical structure. Formal power refers to authority defined as an attribute of the organizational structure and position in the hierarchy.[1] A person in a position of authority has the power granted by status. Ill-exercised power may force and even intimidate followers into obeying instructions. Intimidation comes in several forms: a manager who criticizes in public the report of a follower; a member of the organization who is systematically ignored; and assigning tasks that are impossible to do. In response, followers agree to comply even against their will because they know that they are vulnerable unless they decide to leave the organization.

Therefore, the first formal power source is the organizational hierarchy that gives a person the authority to evaluate followers' performance and set rewards. A person with corporate power sets the agenda for committee meetings, controls scarce resources and investments, and knows the rules and processes used in the organization. Additionally, there are normative powers in comptrollers and prosecutors' offices in public institutions and private companies and in collegiate bodies responsible for defining organizational procedures and rules. Experts also have formal power from knowledge, experience and skills in specialized subjects. Finally, access to unique information is a primary source of formal power.

The traditional image of power where supervisors force people to do things even against their will is not acceptable in Sensible Leadership. This abusive form of power is practiced by ruthless individuals who manipulate followers when assigning work and responsibilities. They can make decisions that can significantly affect organizational culture and wellbeing in the workplace. The concept refers to abusive and rude persons who are dominant and vindictive and use power as a primitive form of domination.

Kramer (2006) offers a vision of "intimidating leaders" that contrast with the fundamental principles of Human Centered Management. Their *political intelligence* doesn't align with their Emotional Intelligence. They do not hesitate to remove obstacles that prevent them from achieving their vision or take advantage of people's weaknesses and insecurities using intimidation and coercive power. Their view of people is instrumental, and they lack empathy for others. Their behavior is confrontational.

The use of power can impact positively or negatively, depending on the way it is exercised. The proper use of formal power can certainly be a source of growth and development and is not necessarily associated with aggressiveness or deceit.

This description of the abusive use of formal power by *intimidating leaders* facilitates understanding and marks differences from a sensible leader who uses *subtle power* to influence followers.

Subtle Power

Sensible Leadership is conceived in this book as a process of significant influence[2] over employees to overcome barriers and promote behaviors to advance the organization's mission and goals.

Getting the willing cooperation and engagement of people is the only way to lead. John Kotter put it clearly when saying that he doesn't like hearing that the only important thing is to maximize shareholders' profits: "when trying to get the cooperation of multiple groups of people, including supervisors, employees, customers, suppliers, and unions, is an infinitely more difficult task than extracting money from businesses".

When sensible leaders exert power over followers, this power is exercised in a *subtle* way, using Emotional Intelligence, emotional influence, trust and positive incentives to advance meaningful organizational projects.

While formal power is based on a highly defined hierarchical structure, orderly tasks, organizational positions, social networks and value chains, *subtle power* focuses on motivating people and engaging them to advance the corporate mission and increase wellbeing. Sensible leaders create a work environment that promotes achievement and generously recognizes followers for accomplishments. They encourage personal development and foster perceptions of self-worth and self-efficacy.

Sensible Leadership exercises subtle power. It differentiates from formal power as an imposition that forces people to carry out activities, even against their will. Followers perceive the use of subtle power as an invitation to participate in appealing and meaningful institutional projects. They feel interested, enthusiastic and are willing to commit their participation without mediating obligations or constraints.

A primary source of subtle power is charisma. Captivating persons are natural leaders. The attractiveness of their personality and ethical behavior inspires confidence and generates enthusiasm. Moreover, their ability to connect emotionally, establish empathetic relationships, and sympathy for others makes them accessible and encourages familiarity, facilitating open, honest and loyal relationships.

Another source of subtle power is genuineness, legitimacy and consistency of leaders' behavior with the organization's values and principles. Leaders are custodians of organizational traditions that guide members, shaping culture and forms of thinking and behavior.

A third source of subtle power is to be recognized as a trustworthy person who will do what it takes to get the job done, particularly in environments subject to change and high uncertainty.

Finally, networks of personal relations are also a source of subtle power that supports leaders.

The Six Principles of Persuasion

"No leader can succeed without mastering the art of persuasion." Hence the importance of understanding the fundamental principles of "the art of persuasion" using subtle power (Cialdini 2006, 2001). The six principles are discussed below:

The Principle of Mutual Appreciation ("Liking")

"People feel more appreciated by those who have similar interests and share preferences." When looking for relationships, the starting point is discovering things in common. Affinity brings people together around issues of mutual interest. The key is creating relationships bonded in mutual respect between leader and follower. Activities can improve when trust and friendship facilitate collaboration. Sincere admiration and praise for others' achievements are expressions of real feelings that make leaders more open and less apprehensive.

The Principle of Reciprocity

"People give back what they receive." Leaders influence followers through personal behavior as role models, creating relationships based on trust, showing a spirit of cooperation and behaving gently. A general tendency among people is to give back what they receive. Helping someone in need increases the chances of getting help when needed. The rule is "give back what you want to receive" or "treat as you want to be treated".

The Principle of Affinity

"It is easier for people to accept guidance and direction from others when there are perceptions of similarities." Leaders' influence over followers is not always direct and obvious but may indirectly affect behaviors through other individuals in the organization. Persuasion by similar people can be compelling coming from peers.

The Principle of Consistency

"People strive to behave in manners consistent with the commitments they make." Leaders influence people to commit to their proposals. When a public position on an issue is freely assumed, people are bound to comply, affecting their behavior. For this reason, followers make commitments that are clear, explicit, formal and known to many people.

The Principle of Authority

"People generally accept the judgment of experts." Disruptions of the global VUCA environment are complex and challenging and often require the support of experts. Medical and health issues are the domain of experts, and the same happens in technology, legal, financial and the social sciences.

Individuals who assume leadership positions based on their expertise must ensure that followers are informed and recognize their qualifications and credentials. Expert leaders earn credibility and reputation that stems from their status as specialists. They need to talk about their backgrounds and experiences relevant to their position, demonstrating effectiveness in problem-solving and avoiding appearing arrogant and superior. When other people in the organization understand and appreciate a leader's expertise, which may not be evident, then expert leaders demonstrate the art of persuasion.

The Scarcity Principle

"People want more of what they have less." People are naturally more attracted to what they have less or to rare and unique opportunities. The economic value of scarcity is related to this principle of human nature. When products or services are hard to get, they look more appealing. If things appear limited, they induce a psychological feeling of regret that makes people show a higher preference for them. Hence the use of great deals, bargains and unique offers for a limited time or in limited quantities "subject to availability in stock" appeals to this principle. But what is said must be valid and reliable; otherwise, credibility is lost, and trust is eroded due to unethical behaviors. Leaders who share benefits or information with followers, gain committed and active responses.

Notes

1 In colloquial terms, the source of authority stems from the organizational hierarchy position. But it may also come from people's recognition, as in the case of an expert in a subject who is a *technical authority*, while a captivating person is a *charismatic authority*.
2 The influence of one party over others requires some degree of dependency (large or small, unilateral or reciprocal) between them. Otherwise, there is no possibility of persuasion or control (Weberian postulate).

References

Cialdini, R. (2001). Harnessing the science of persuasion. *Harvard Business Review*, October, 72–79.
Cialdini, R. (2006). *Influence: The Psychology of Persuasion*. New York, NY: Collins Business Essentials, Harper Collins.
Kramer, R. (2006). The great intimidators. *Harvard Business Review*, February, 88–96.
Weber, M., Henderson, A. M., and Talcott, P. (1947). *The Theory of Social and Economic Organization*. New York, NY: Oxford University Press.

7 Influence through Communication

Communication is the most effective tool leaders use to influence followers. Leaders use *formal* and *subtle* approaches to communicate with employees. Formal systems, like organizational structure, management control and incentives, are *means of communication* affecting people's behavior and corporate culture. Changes like adjustments to the organizational structure, redefinition of budgets, new performance measurements and compensation changes communicate messages with substantial symbolic meaning. Leaders cannot openly speak their minds because their actions and what they say are interpreted as reflections of their intentions.

Formal approaches are incomplete without considering that *formal communications* have a subtle component that cannot be ignored. The art of leading requires a deep awareness of the symbolic value of actions and decisions.

Inspiring leaders rely highly on subtle communication. They clearly show that workers are *building a cathedral* not just *chopping stones*. Leaders have the vital responsibility to help people understand the meaning of their work, sharing visions, and doing their best to achieve what they have planned. They must feel proud to be part of a community, share the same ideals, and do their best to achieve what they have set out to do. In the process, leaders gain credibility and the trust of followers.

The strategic project must be told as a good story, attractive, challenging, appealing, inviting coworkers to be part of the adventure. The story's parts and elements form an integrated whole (Brown, Bromiley, and Shaw, 1998). It is the pure and straightforward communication of the company's *dream*. The leader cannot delegate this task.

Compelling communication of the leader's vision enhances the meaning of work and life. Communication helps people understand what they are doing, find meaning in their effort and enrich their job. They get motivated because they appreciate the work they do.

Sensible leaders need to motivate workers who arrive to work eager for the time to go by and leave work to run home. When employees lack motivation, they are unable to be engaged with their job because the organizational environment is contrary to personal development and growth. In these cases, the waste of human talent and corporate resources can reach harmful proportions. Most often, the root of these problems stems from dysfunctional communication channels and ineffective organizational programs.

Moreover, communications help leaders relate to external audiences and move in the political environment. It is necessary to bring together very diverse interests to promote the organization's vision; to seduce, negotiate and convince, appealing not only to minds but overall, to *hearts*.

The importance of communication skills in modern organizations is covered extensively in the complementary book *Soft Skills in Human Centered Management: A Global Perspective* (Lepeley, Beutell, Abarca, and Majluf, 2021) in this Human Centered Management Trilogy. Communications are essential to consolidate the "Resilience – Agility Umbrella" (Lepeley, 2021) that provides the analytical framework for a growing number of Soft Skills people use to advance human relations in the family, education, social life and the workplace.

Leading is Communicating

Entering the world of communication is stepping into a genuinely subtle world. Leaders need to explain the organizational mission to motivate followers. Still, they must enticingly deliver messages to communicate effectively and make sure that those receiving the message decipher original intentions and are affected in their minds, emotions and affections.

Effective communications involve complex mental processes and emotions. Therefore, as leading spokespersons, leaders need to be articulate, persuasive and speak with transparency and truth. Sensible leaders communicate fluidly and clearly.

Leaders need to be analytically competent and excel in math and numbers as most leaders base their decisions and actions on rigorous analysis. When leaders have access to data, they can confront myths, rumors and speculations with self-assurance and a clear rationale based on objective analysis. But that is not enough. Leaders also need to have a compelling story to tell their followers about their vision of the organization. The data analysis may appeal to reason but can hardly reach emotions and hearts, which are essential to motivate people and engage employees with effective communications. Management is about making decisions and executing specific actions but doing so with enthusiasm and energy.

Leaders and followers find the meaning at work when organizational stories are forceful and persuasive. The key is not only to communicate but to communicate effectively. The message and the narrative must be coherent, credible, honest and enticing. Communications must be open, and those who tell it must be credible. Leaders must show coherence between what they say and do because body language, attitudes and actions always convey the real meaning and cannot be silenced.

Storytelling and Effective Communications

Traditionally storytelling has been an essential part of family gatherings. Most people grew up listening to grandparents' stories recounting memorable anecdotes about their lives, experiences and values that touch their hearts and become unforgettable. This common situation is a clear example of the importance of narratives that define family identity.

Stories shared across generations are central to strengthening organizational culture and constitute an essential pillar of the collective heritage. These stories repeated over time are a powerful means to preserve the historical context and share with newcomers cultural traditions, because past lessons illuminate the present and serve as guides for the future. Stories communicate values, define ethos and differentiate organizational character through vivid accounts transmitted from leaders to coworkers and from person to person. Thus, new hires entering the organization become part of the *shared purpose* embedded in Human Centered Organizational Culture (Lepeley, Morales, Essens, Beutell, and Majluf, 2021).

Organizational stories are powerful learning experiences for people. They convey the organization's knowledge implicit in the structure, strategies and processes embedded in its culture. So, when telling stories, it is important to communicate values, attitudes and behaviors the organization promotes as integral parts of its history and culture, reflected in its mission and vision. Narratives show new hires the traditional and distinctive ways of living and looking at realities not included in other work experiences.

Organizational stories are valuable not only when told for the first time but also when retold as they become part of the cultural heritage (Brown and Duguid, 2000). In organizations, people often narrate stories and give different interpretations that shape tradition, establish values and redefine the organizational vision (Boje, 1995). Corporate sagas facilitate understanding of the culture, provide meaning to shared experiences and renew a sense of purpose, generating commitment to the shared project and vision (Boyce, 1996; Fleming, 2001; McKee, 1997; Parkin, 2004). These stories awaken emotions and help interpret events that mold people's experiences because images and metaphors influence people's engagement with work, contributing to personal growth and improvement of organizational values (Kaye, 1996).

When organizations face disruptions and change that introduce uncertainty and fear in the workplace, organizational narratives can provide continuity to foster resilience and agility to communicate that change and transformation can be successful regardless of how radical it may seem.

Kolb, in his article "Seeking continuity amidst organizational change: A storytelling approach" in the *Journal of Management Inquiry* (2003), conveys the power of narrative telling about the experience of Amcor, an Australian global packaging company. In one year, Amcor implemented five changes simultaneously, ranging from risk prevention in the assembly line to adjustments in work shifts and a new incentive program. During a workshop, where 30 employees participated, the consultants asked the oldest member to describe Amcor's position when he decided to work for the company. They then asked the same thing to the employee who preceded him in seniority, continuing until all 30 employees told their story. The anecdotes were full of humor and laughter and rarely included bitterness or complaints. The goal was to connect old employees with new hires, leading to discovering that what most believed in was a *new way* to do things that were not really *new*. Although not identical to previous experiences, employees found that the proposed changes were not more challenging than the changes they had already successfully undergone in the past. This process helped new employees value older employees' experiences who "had been there and done this". The result was that by telling these stories, the employees broadened their perspective and reduced their resistance to change.

Communication experts expressing their views in HBR articles, such as Denning's (2004) "Telling Tales" and Morgan's (2008) "How to become an authentic speaker", have emphasized storytelling for effective communications.

In organizations, leaders need to tell stories with a passion for showing an enticing vision of the future. Sensible Leadership is about inspiring coworkers to act effectively in difficult situations, often in uncommon ways. The information is remembered more accurately and quickly when presented in the form of examples or stories that are captivating and entertaining, not purely using the *precision of numbers*.

Trying to convince people through statistics or PowerPoint slides will not achieve this goal. Doing it through storytelling often does. In fact, in certain situations, no other method would work.

A research study compared the effectiveness of four different ways to persuade MBA students about an unlikely hypothesis that the firm practiced, *avoiding layoffs*. The first method was to tell a story. In the second, researchers provided statistical data. In the third, they provided statistical information and a story. In the fourth, they asked a former company executive to present the policy of the company. The most effective method turned out to be the first one, which relies only on telling a story (Abarca, 2010).

Leaders must be proficient and credible communicators, which is easier to say than to achieve. An essential condition is having consistency between verbal and nonverbal language, words and body expressions, and content and gestures that complement messages.

Inspiring communicators convey real passion for a subject, manifest enthusiasm, and present ideas lucidly, logically and clearly. Moreover, they prepare and adapt stories to listeners, can connect effectively with audiences and adjust their delivery along the presentation to address peoples' reactions. Effective communicators know the power of narratives to motivate people. Cold numbers can stimulate reason but can hardly move, galvanize or stir people's attention. Leaders need the ability to build stories appropriate for the circumstances to achieve the intended objectives. Denning (2004) identifies the following ways to tell the story: moving to action, presenting oneself, transmitting values, promoting followers, facing rumors, sharing knowledge and guiding people into the future.

Communication and Interpersonal Relations

Communication is a central human activity and the basis of interpersonal relationships. People use different kinds of communication processes to understand each other. Mutual influences become unavoidable in this exchange process. People learn how other people see them and get a fairer personal assessment. Many individual needs become apparent when relating to others.

It would not be an exaggeration to say that communications occur even if people have no intentions to communicate. In fact, *living implies communicating* because people are always communicating with other people. Human communication ranges from primitive, like movements and sounds, to most elaborate, based on words and symbols representing objects or ideas.

People's social nature makes them interdependent, always seeking communications with others, and exchanging messages to understand perceptions, ideas and experiences. Communication is one of the central skills in the development of Emotional Intelligence and, consequently, it is a crucial ability for leaders to relate to and influence followers.

Most employees indicate that one of the main problems they face in organizations is communication, despite evidence that leaders devote over 80 percent of their time to improve communications. Moreover, organizations allocate a substantial amount of resources to this effort. Communication is essential to expedite organizational life. The ability to communicate face-to-face has a high impact on promotions and future success. A sample of employees from 88 organizations showed that interpersonal communication skills were rated the most important out of 31 skills in the survey (Abarca, 2010).

Communication is not a simple matter, and in fact, many barriers obstruct effective communications. Communication problems may arise when writing, sending or receiving messages, demanding persistent efforts to ensure effective communication, and avoiding obstacles that impair clarity and easy understanding. Typical misinterpretations occur when messages are incomplete, unclear or inappropriate to the situation. Also, messages can be ignored or distorted by biased interpretations and mental frameworks. In a survey of 13,000 people in universities, military units, government agencies and hospitals, almost all respondents thought they were better at communicating than other individuals (Abarca, 2010).

Furthermore, communication is not an isolated event but commonly involves continuous interactions that change how people feel or think according to the feedback received. Breakdowns typically occur in complex and sustained processes ending in misunderstandings or conflict between parties because most people believe that communication problems are due to the other part's failures.

Finally, leadership calls for the most careful and effective forms of communication because leaders' behavior and decisions are spelled out in messages that people have to understand and decipher. A sensible leader leads by example, and the first component of good communication is credibility and trust. Leaders must pay special attention to critical decisions' communicational content, such as organizational structure changes, pressure for deadlines and consistency between their actions and the corporate values and mission (Ham, 2006).

The following are relevant attributes of effective communications that leaders must consider in dealing with followers:

- *Be clear; avoid generalities.* Avoid using general terms such as "most people" or "some of our friends", since unspecific terms are difficult to understand and conceal messages.
- *Be precise.* Include only necessary information in messages, use framework references and spell out basic assumptions to facilitate correct understanding. For example, give clear work instructions and a realistic description of what collaborators must do. New employees especially appreciate accurate information.
- *Define communication objectives explicitly.* The goal of communication is to influence, inform and express emotions. If the specific aim is to *influence*, state this before providing details.
- *Secure consistency between verbal and nonverbal messages.* Face-to-face communications involve verbal and nonverbal messages, for instance, when people say they are happy and are simultaneously smiling and expressing their wellbeing in other nonverbal ways. Contradictory verbal and nonverbal messages are confusing.
- *Be redundant in communication.* Communicate not once, but many times. Repeat messages using different approaches to secure understanding (drawings, nonverbal expressions, written statements).
- *Give and ask for feedback.* Give people specific and descriptive feedback on positive evaluations, identify areas of improvement, focus on actions and avoid making people feel guilty or ashamed. Recognize merit when necessary.
- *Ask for feedback on how people receive the message and verify that everybody understands, especially when expressing emotions.* Communication problems arise from different interpretations people give to the same message. Hence it is important to ask direct questions to ensure communications came across as intended. Do not just ask,

"do you have any doubts?" It is essential to use feedback to learn if messages are understood correctly.

- *Adapt the message to the audience.* Explaining a topic to an expert or a novice, a child or an adult requires different approaches.
- *Use diverse ways to communicate feelings.* Use examples, metaphors or representative actions to express feelings and emotions.
- *Build empathy.* Make people feel comfortable. Start the communication with a brief talk related to the message to prepare the person to receive it. And when referring to the behavior of other people, be cautious to avoid hurting sensibilities. Use descriptions over evaluations.
- *Take care of relationships.* Show openness and warmth in communications to express care and concern for collaborators' well-being, pointing out they are valued and esteemed.
- *Achieve commitment and make sure to follow up.* When the communication objective is to inform or express emotions, there is no need to define commitments. However, when the goal is to influence other people, it is necessary to formalize agreements with clear responsibilities, defining actions and milestones for effective follow-up.
- *Spread organization news in a timely way* using technology, social media, emails, websites, CCTV (closed-circuit television) among others.

Virtual Communication and the Loss of the Human Moment

The *human moment* is a psychological encounter that happens when two people share the same physical space (Hallowell, 1999). The influence of technology and the internet impairs the human moment, which is increasingly rare today and disappearing in modern life. Hallowell noted two decades ago, the destructive dimension of the absence of the human moment. Evidence of this is increasingly apparent as people worldwide are being subject to prolonged lockdowns, social distancing and teleworking imposed by the 2020 coronavirus global pandemic. Communication in organizations is increasingly taking place through voice mail, email and other virtual messaging systems displacing personal contact and altering the human moment. The progressive disappearance of human moments reveals detrimental consequences that include increased sensitivity, sense of isolation and feelings of ailing, resulting in lower work engagement levels, job satisfaction, performance and productivity that hinder long-term organizational sustainability.

Hallowell stated that the human moment when communicating has two prerequisites: physical presence and emotional and intellectual attention. Sometimes a five-minute engaged conversation can have a significant meaning for people.

Face-to-face interactions are essential to stimulate emotional well-being and intellectual activity and acuteness. Communicating through email misses important nonverbal components that infuse meaning to a message, mainly body language, voice tones and facial expressions that capture unique subtleties like wit, humor and other signs of care and warmth. This assertion does not intend to diminish the value of virtual communications but emphasizes that they are not perfect substitutes for human contact. Face-to-face interactions remain vital in organizations, especially in tech organizations, prone to rely only on remote work.

Communication Happens in Many Ways

Management is communication and leaders need to be effective communicators verbally and nonverbally. Leaders have to use the power of words and gestures, and what they do or do not do are also powerful forms of communication because often, "actions speak louder than words". Leaders also use corporate events, publications in newspapers, magazines and electronic media to communicate.

Messages need to be direct and credible and must be delivered using different means and often repeated, emphasizing old points and new information. Not all people understand the expected intention and intensity of messages, and information is easy to forget. Moreover, people in an organization are diverse. They may interpret messages in very different ways, for instance, men and women, young and older, experts and apprentices, managers and employees, or specialists in technical matters vs. personal relationships. Therefore, sensible leaders communicate using many different voices and nonverbal clues.

Communications have symbolic value transmitted through words, body language or nonverbal communication, images and actions.

Words: Verbal Communication

Leaders spend about 50 percent of their time in verbal communications, assuming that their messages are clear and accurate. But this is not necessarily the case. The meaning of words is not an intrinsic characteristic, but it is an attribution of people. A word hardly has the same meaning for two people. They interpret messages differently according to their backgrounds and experiences.

Moreover, the meaning of a word depends on the context. The circumstances in which communication takes place are essential to clarify verbal messages minimizing confusion. For instance, it is different saying, "let's meet tomorrow" than "given what we have advanced today defining the problem, let's meet tomorrow at 3 p.m. in my office to close the subject".

Widespread perception exercises show that meaning depends on the context. For instance, in Figure 7.1, the middle symbol may be interpreted as a number or a letter. For "the horizontals", it is a number, but for "the verticals", a letter.

Figure 7.1 Meaning Depends on Context.

Successful communicators focus on ideas rather than words because people assign meaning to words depending on personal experience and history. For instance, a young adult's interpretation that attending a party requires "formal dress" is very different from an older person's understanding.

Meaning is inseparable from people's life stories. All words are associated with memories, feelings and other nuances that influence personal intents. When people communicate, the meaning of words may not correspond to conventional dictionary definitions but personal interpretations. As writer Julio Cortázar (1963) said, "language is residing in a particular reality", a very relevant issue when communicating to avoid misunderstandings.

Nonverbal Communications

The impression a person has of others in social interactions is influenced significantly by nonverbal clues, particularly by *body language*. Nonverbal clues include face gestures, hand movements, attention when listening, smiles, posture, walking or sitting down, tone of voice, social distancing, eye contact, greeting traditions, among many others.

Nonverbal expressions say a great deal about people, their appreciation of a particular subject, and their state of mind. For instance, surprise appears in the face, pleasure in a smile and displeasure in voice tone. They are uncontrollable gestures and reactions that show up as a *silent choir* that is inaudible but actually is *singing at the top of the lungs*. The first axiom of communication is then: "it is impossible not to communicate" because nonverbal clues can speak louder and clearer than verbal utterances. Words only tell one part of the story, a minor one.

Albert Merhabian (1981), emeritus professor of psychology at the University of California, Los Angeles, is well known for enhancing the importance of nonverbal messages. He is the author of the "7%-38%-55% Rule". Accordingly, 55 percent of a presenter's impact is body language, including posture, gestures, eye contact, 38 percent being the tone of voice, and only 7 percent the presentation's content. Expressions such as "I can tell by the way you walk" show the extent to which people are giving and receiving information in social relations even when they are unaware.

Darioly and Mast (2014) present an integrative view of the role of nonverbal behavior in leadership in the Routledge edited book *Leader Interpersonal and Influence Skills: The Soft Skills of Leadership* by Riggio and Tan. Their study supports the importance of nonverbal clues in leadership and confirms that although words are important, they only tell one part of the story.

Understanding and managing nonverbal language is undoubtedly a powerful Soft Skill for improving communications and interpersonal relationships. Leaders need to place special attention on synchronizing words with body language. When words say one thing and the body another, there is a mismatch in communications usually resolved in favor of body language because it is more difficult to control and reveals real thoughts and feelings. It is not possible to simulate nonverbal communication. Personal feelings and intentions will inevitably come into sight.

Consistency between verbal and nonverbal language indicates that a person is genuine and trustworthy, facilitating social relationships. Inconsistencies create tensions. Yet the perception of nonverbal messages plays tricks because interpretations are not always evident or clear. It is a process embedded in a high degree of subjectivity, so there are occasions when nonverbal message interpretations may lead to misunderstandings.

Images: "A Picture is Worth a Thousand Words"

Images are a powerful language of communication with high symbolic content. Images are widely used by leaders to convey information about the present and the future of an organization.

Images are abstract representations of simple or complex ideas. Images are used even to represent an organization's strategy in a metaphorical form. For instance, a management team that needs to develop and present a written mission statement will formally approach the task. Alternatively, if the team has to represent the organizational mission in a picture or play, the result may be quite different, and team members' input can be surprising (Gosling and Mintzberg, 2004). The same happens when a team has to write a marketing strategy "to give customers the best shopping experience" or select a representative image showing a smiling person who welcomes customers with a polite and kind gesture. Words and pictures are two different, but complementary ways to convey a message.

The use of images makes it clear that *language* is not limited to words. It may also include photographs and illustrations that *tell the story* in different ways, with multiple interpretations depending on the audience. This form of communication opens wider opportunities for the message to be understood by a broader audience, with varied skills, and it is more likely to be remembered.

A good communication exercise to transmit ideas to an audience is a PowerPoint presentation that combines words and images. Preparing the presentation requires designing slides and choosing pictures and sentences to facilitate information understanding by the audience, and its retention, ideally, for a long time. For instance, a slide with too many words is less effective than a concise sentence with a few meaningful words that can communicate a vast amount of information. Alternatively, the information may be conveyed effectively through stunning pictures grasped by the audience. But it is an even better practice to use the same image with a short clarifying sentence to avoid subjective interpretations far removed from the message's intent.

Action: "By their Deeds, They Shall be Known"

The familiar adage "actions speak louder than words" indicates that a person communicates more effectively through meritorious actions and behaviors than giving self-indulgent speeches. Words are not needed when doing the right thing.

Actions are a powerful language for everybody, especially for leaders to communicate with followers. Actions are always significant and have implications of ethical behavior. Trustworthy leaders earn followers' trust with their daily behavior, not by repeating the organization's code of ethics. It is better to act with truth and justice than to say that the two primary principles of the organization that everybody must practice and live by are truth and justice. The most effective form of influencing followers is the consistency of leaders' behavior. Leaders may send contradictory messages when they say one thing and do another. People in general and employees in particular trust actions more than words. Building credibility takes many years, but it can be lost in a minute of misbehaving. Low credibility creates severe communication problems.

Lastly, inactions also transmit symbolic messages because acting and not acting imply communication, regardless of the intention. For instance, leaders who express recognition for a job well done are encouraging followers. Lack of merit recognition sends a message even without saying any word or taking any action. In this case, it is a discouraging message.

Considering that communication credibility rests on truthfulness, experience and dynamism, leaders must act with integrity, speak from a solid knowledge base and communicate messages with enthusiasm.

References

Abarca, N. (2010). *The leader as a coach (El líder como coach)*. Santiago, Chile: El Mercurio Aguilar.

Boje, D. (1995). Stories of the storytelling organization: a postmodern analysis of Disney as 'Tamara-land'. *Academy of Management Journal*, 38, 997–1035.

Boyce, M. E. (1996). Organizational story and storytelling: a critical review. *Journal of Organizational Change Management*, 9(5), 5.

Brown, J. S., and Duguid, P. (2000). *The Social Life of Information*. Boston, MA: Harvard Business School Press.

Brown, R., Bromiley, P., and Shaw, G. (1998). Strategic stories: how M is rewriting business planning. *Harvard Business Review*, May-June, 41–50.

Cortázar, J. (1963). *Rayuela*, Paris and Buenos Aires: Pantheon Books p.351. Retrieved   http://web.seducoahuila.gob.mx/biblioweb/upload/Cortazar,%20 Julio%20-%20Rayuela.pdf

Darioly, A., and Mast, M. S. (2014). The role of nonverbal behavior in leadership: An integrative review. In R. E. Riggio & S. J. Tan (Eds.), *Leadership: Research and Practice. Leader Interpersonal and Influence Skills: The Soft Skills of Leadership*. Routledge/Taylor & Francis Group, 73–100. Retrieved https://psycnet.apa.org/record/2013-43045-004

Denning, S. (2004). Telling tales. *Harvard Business Review*, May, 122–129.

Fleming, D. (2001). Narrative leadership: using the power of stories. *Strategy & Leadership*, 29(4), 34.

Gosling, J., and Mintzberg, H. (2004). The education of practicing managers. *MIT Sloan Management Review*, Summer.

Hallowell, E. M. (1999). The human moment at work. *Harvard Business Review*, January–February, 58–66.

Ham, J. (2006). The five messages leaders must manage. *Harvard Business Review*, May, 114–123.

Kaye, M. (1996). *Mythmakers and Story-tellers*. Melbourne: Business and Professional Publishing.

Kolb, D. G. (2003). Seeking continuity amidst organizational change: a storytelling approach. *Journal of Management Inquiry*, 12(2), 180–183.

Lepeley, M. T. (2021), Soft Skills: the lingua franca of Human Centered Management in the global VUCA environment, in Lepeley, M.T., Beutell, N., Abarca, N., Majluf, N. (eds.). *Soft Skills for Human Centered Management and Global Sustainability*, Routledge.

Lepeley, M. T., Beutell, N., Abarca, N., and Majluf, N. (eds.). (2021). *Soft Skills for Human Centered Management and Global Sustainability*, Routledge.

Lepeley, M. T., Morales, O., Essens, P., Beutell, N., and Majluf, N., (eds.). (2021). *Human Centered Organizational Culture: Global Dimensions*. Routledge.

McKee, R. (1997). *Story: Substance, Structure, Style and the Principles of Screenwriting 1*. New York. NY: Regan Books.

Merhabian, A. (1981). *Silent Messages: Implicit Communication of Emotions and Attitudes*. 2nd ed. Belmont, Calif., Wadsworth.

Morgan, N. (2008). How to become an authentic speaker. *Harvard Business Review*, November, 115–119.

Parkin, M. (2004). *Tales for Change: Using Storytelling to Develop People and Organizations*. London: Kogan Page.

8 Conflict Management and Negotiation Talent
Two Essential Leadership Skills

Conflict among individuals is inevitable in organizations, then negotiation and agreements are essential to foster progress. The outcome of conflict may be positive or negative; therefore, effective conflict management is necessary to facilitate organizational development and create a stimulating climate.

Conflicts are common; solving them is essential, and leaders play a critical role in the outcome. When conflicts arise, leaders must manage them towards favorable outcomes for all the persons and parties involved to help develop people, teams and the organization (Fisher, Ury, and Patton, 2011).

Recurrent and unsolved conflicts may be a sign of more profound constraints that can damage relationships and break work teams. Sensible leaders anticipate the occurrence of disputes and prepare the organization to benefit instead of losing from them, using differences among people as opportunities to improve results and avoid the emergence of more severe problems. Leaders may even strategically create crises as instruments to advance change and innovation.

The Inevitability of Conflicts

Conflict is a constant in human relations and inherent in all interactions. Conflicts arise because different people, with different experiences and backgrounds, each see and understand the world in varying ways (*cognitive differentiation*), and often have conflicting interests.

Conflicts can take place among different actors and at different levels. For instance, they may emerge at the personal level, between teams, between units in an organization or with other organizations. Within an organization, conflicts arise when people, groups or divisions pursue different goals or objectives. They may have different priorities on various issues, such as allocating resources and scheduling, or maybe the targets of one work unit depend on another unit's outcome, increasing work complexity and making coordination harder. Consequently, it is relevant to identify from the beginning if the causes of the conflict are rational motives, such as failures in logistics, or emotional reasons, like blaming people for inconsistencies.

Conflict management acknowledges that the same fact or situation is often interpreted differently by different people or parties and may not have the same importance or meaning. Discrepancies in assessment and opposing interests are the rule more than the exception. Yet not all conflicts are harmful, and most of all, it is possible and beneficial to learn from the difficulties.

A well-managed conflict provides valuable opportunities for people to gain knowledge, experience and skills in different matters. When people and organizations take conflicts as an exogenous variable or an unusual incident, they ignore fundamental social and organizational developments. Moreover, they waste valuable opportunities for improvement and personal learning and growth.

A significant issue here is that people and organizations need to understand that conflict management can bring potential benefits and make efforts to learn from disputes and expected difficulties that affect people and organizations. There are relevant differences between *conflicts, dysfunctional conflicts* and destructive fighting.

Rational and Emotional Dimensions of Conflict

In conflicts, it is necessary to recognize rational and emotional components. The rational component is based on differences in the analysis of an issue, for instance, defining a plan for introducing a new product to the market. While some people may prefer to start with a pilot plan applied to only one region, to test results before expanding to other territories, another group may choose to conduct a massive national effort. Here, the conflict's rational component relates to disagreements about marketing strategy and different assumptions about the best way to launch the product. This disagreement is healthy and essential to refine plans to attract human talent and optimize resources. But conflicts also have emotional components driven by human nature, like personal interests, preferences or antagonisms with the potential to escalate and lead to confrontations, rivalries and quarrels interfering in interpersonal relationships. When controversy between the negotiating parties increases, they are less willing to cooperate in resolving the conflict. Emotions are an inherent component of disputes and have emotional implications for all the people involved (Kimberlyn, Pillemer, and Wheeler, 2013).

Conflicts are a significant and usual test for leaders, who need to demonstrate capacity as effective mediators between conflicting parties while avoiding an overflow of emotions that may prevent attaining the best decisions. However, leaders need to be aware that emotions are an inevitable dimension in conflicts and negotiations. Therefore, conflict management needs to balance a rational exchange of ideas and deal effectively with negotiators' emotions.

A rational debate characterizes a well-managed conflict. The alternatives are deeply analyzed, and the discussion and solutions that satisfy each party develop as carefully controlled interactions. Leaders must make sure that managing a conflict promptly and dealing with it effectively is a constructive opportunity to move forward, avoiding setbacks for people and the organization.

In this book, the definition of conflict includes a rational and an emotional dimension. Leaders act both as mediators or facilitators of contrasting views of persons or parties and handle the emotions involved in decisions or agreements. When leaders fail to manage and regulate emotions, the atmosphere may turn antagonistic, and even if the right decision is reached, it is not easy to implement. Proper handling of a conflict's rational and emotional facets leads to organizational improvement anchored in better decisions, contributing to high performance and long-term sustainability.

Sources and Stages in a Conflict Process

Conflicts do not appear suddenly; they often manifest in the last stage of a long incubation process of divergences and differences between individuals, teams or organizations (Pondy, 1967; Fisher, Ury, and Patton, 2011).

Sources of Conflict

Within organizations, conflicts are often identified as communication problems, though they may also result from structural or personal variables. Different sources of conflict are listed below (Abarca, 2017).

Communication Problems

Lack of effective communication is the most common source leading to interpersonal conflicts and can lead to situations difficult to solve. Explaining conflicts as a *communication problem* is not surprising because every person understands and interprets reality differently. Moreover, those who receive the message can interpret them differently and wonder: "what are they trying to tell me?"

Frequently, communication problems originate in misunderstandings or different perceptions according to personal experiences and expectations. The perceptions of life and the surrounding environment are selective and intimate. Walter Lippmann wrote: *"we are all captive of the images in our minds and the belief that what we experience is the world that exists"* (Morrow, 1985).

Conflict may also arise when one person or party attributes devious intentions to others. When an interpersonal relationship weakens and trust is lost, communication ceases to be functional. Any relationship maintained over time requires trust. When confidence is impaired, the risk of conflict has a higher potential to escalate.

Communication constraints become severe when accentuated by differences in structures, personalities and personal values that complicate interpersonal relationships and generate conflicts.

Structural Variables

These refer to issues such as how an organization works, how tasks, roles and individual responsibilities are assigned, and the relations between the different departments. These structural differences have the potential to generate personal or organizational conflicts.

Another recurrent source of conflict is associated with organizational change. It arises when people in different positions of responsibility or holding contradicting points of view disagree on what, when, how or why to perform specific tasks, on the best way to use resources or the work needed to achieve defined objectives.

Personal interests and other issues emerge when organizations change people's positions, status or compensation. Threats to *personal status* resulting from organizational change are a source of conflict when employees feel negatively affected and try to defend their situation against those who put them at risk.

Structural conflicts are particularly common in mergers and acquisitions, especially in international and global cases dealing with cultural differences.

Personal Variables

These include people's personality, economic, social and value differences. *Personality* refers to the relatively stable patterns of behavior, attitudes and needs. Conflicts arise from *personality clashes*, when there are disagreements, and people are not inclined to seek solutions to reach mutual benefits, ignoring other people's interests and needs. Some individuals do not get along with each other and sometimes reasons are difficult to decipher.

Often conflicts among people originate in social groups to which they belong. As a result, friction may increase due to social and physical differences such as race, religion, sex, age, marital status and income. Differences in the value system are a significant source of conflict. Values refer to ethics and perceptions of what is right, desirable or appropriate. Beliefs and personal philosophies drive people to different points of view, confronting challenging situations and decisions. Conflicts are more difficult to address when associated with subjective matters of disagreements than with objective issues such as product design or the definition of a promotional campaign.

Although the leading tendency is to attribute conflicts primarily to personal variables, organizational conflict experts consider that the impact of *personal* variables is lower than *structural* or *communicational* variables (Abarca, 2017).

Stages in a Conflict

There are four stages in the conflict process. The first stage is a *potential conflict* that doesn't require urgent attention, at least at the beginning. But if differences prolong over time, the situation becomes progressively difficult and may advance to a *perceived conflict* and later to a *felt conflict*. If the process goes on, it becomes an *overt conflict* either manifest or covert.

Potential conflict is a possibility associated with specific conditions that may trigger conflictive situations, such as weak and inadequate communications, structural and organizational constraints, or personal characteristics and differences among people.

Perceived conflict is increased awareness that a situation may escalate to *overt conflict*. The conflict is more likely to erupt, but whether it escalates depends on the person in charge of monitoring its evolution.

Felt conflict recognizes that the conflict arouses emotions, which need to be addressed as a significant issue. Feelings, such as fear and anger, commonly arise at this stage.

Consequently, conflict resolution depends on the parties identifying the prevailing stage in the conflict's evolution to choose the best course of action. But this step is not enough when the problem is emotionally engaging the parties involved. Conflicts escalate when one party attributes intentions to the other. Perceived and felt conflicts lead to the next stage of *overt conflict*.

Overt conflict takes different forms. From subtle behaviors (*covert conflict*) to open confrontation (*manifest conflict*). There are strategies for resolving overt conflicts that may lead to a positive or negative outcome.

Functional and Dysfunctional Conflicts

Conflicts may be functional or dysfunctional. *Functional conflicts* confronting people or groups may result in benefits for organizational performance. In *dysfunctional conflicts* disputes or interactions between people or groups can harm wellbeing, preventing goal achievements. Therefore, conflicts may end in positive or negative results, depending on how they are handled.

Sensible leaders intervene at the early stages of conflicts when they notice the first signs of a *perceived conflict* or the emotional implications in a *felt conflict* way before the situation escalates to *overt conflict*. They try to channel discrepancies towards a *positive conflict* and avoid the frustration inherent in *negative conflict*.

Positive conflicts provide opportunities for the parties to discuss and share ideas and review the benefits for each party, settling conflicting interests using win-win negotiation techniques to bring together divergent perceptions and preferences (Fisher, Ury, and Patton, 2011). When this happens, conflict becomes an opportunity for collaboration that strengthens wellbeing and long-term organizational sustainability. In this case, the differences that lead to conflict become a source of personal and collective enrichment.

In negative conflicts, results lead to open and profound confrontation loaded with negative emotions and parties feeling resentment and aggressiveness that deteriorate relationships, hinder teamwork and harm organizational climate and culture.

Leaders need to compare the benefits and costs of conflicts resulting from necessary changes and critical innovations. The golden rule is that conflicts can neither be too low nor too high. If the level of conflict is too low, it will be hard to make organizational changes and adapt to trends in markets and the environment, curtailing sustainability and survival. On the other hand, high levels of pervasive conflict lead to chaos and situations that jeopardize productivity and produce permanent harm. Sensible leaders can determine the optimal level of conflict to enhance organizations.

Conflict Resolution Strategies

The strategy leaders use to solve conflicts is considered one of the most relevant factors in their effectiveness assessment. They may use cooperation and competition, significantly affecting the outcome:

- *Competitive Behavior* refers to the extent to which individuals or parties strive to satisfy their interests and objectives *at their counterpart's expense.*
- *Cooperative Behavior* refers to the degree to which individuals or parties strive to satisfy their interests and objectives *jointly with their counterparts.*

Table 8.1 presents a matrix of the two dimensions of behaviors associated with five conflict resolution strategies (Thomas, 1992).

Avoiding Strategy

This strategy is neither competitive nor cooperative. When individuals using this strategy face a conflictive situation, they avoid, deny or evade deciding. They do not assume the conflict. They neither advocate their interest nor that of the counterpart. The conflict is left unresolved, waiting for a better opportunity. Also, when considering the situation threatening, they prefer to withdraw from it.

Table 8.1 Conflict Resolution Strategies in Terms of Two Dimensions: "Competitive Behavior" and "Cooperative Behavior"

		Competitive behavior		
		Low	*Middle*	*High*
Cooperative behavior	*High*	Accommodating		Collaborating
	Middle		Compromising	
	Low	Avoiding		Competing

Avoiding strategies are hardly accepted in conflict resolution. Dodging conflicts tends to harm the leaders' image and effectiveness as unfit to meet challenges, despite the complexity of the tasks at hand. However, it can be an effective strategy in specific situations when the best decision is not to make any decision, as when the conflict is not critical, it does not require immediate attention, or it is a matter better decided by other parties. Avoidance strategy helps delay the decision process and gain extra time to gather information. It also allows cooling down emotions and waiting for better conditions to negotiate to minimize costs and maximize benefits.

Competing Strategy

Conflict resolution rests on competitive behavior without giving too much weight to cooperative behavior. People look for their interests, beliefs and rights at the expense of the counterpart. This strategy seeks the dominance of one party over the other to impose a position. For example, presenting people as experts and using this capacity to enforce strong arguments to win space in a negotiation.

The competitive strategy commonly becomes a confrontation between unyielding positions, as a *matter of principle*. It involves high risks when the parties become hostile and entrenched in inflexible positions obstructing any agreement possibility. If one party always imposes their will, they demotivate the party that yields. The conflict's solution may be the best, but the relationship deteriorates, and motivation to promote new initiatives is lost. It all comes down to one party winning and the other losing.

Accommodating Strategy

The accommodating strategy represents the reverse of the competing strategy. Cooperative behavior prevails, and the interests of both parties are relevant to reach a mutually beneficial outcome. Both parties defer their interests in favor of their counterpart.

In repetitive conflict situations, giving in may be an appropriate strategy when the issue under negotiation is more relevant to one party, making it easier for the other party to concede. In this case, the best solution is to give up in exchange for something crucial that may come in the future.

Accommodating strategy distinguishes between a *forced accommodation*, which leads to the accumulation of resentment by the yielding party, and a *strategic accommodation* in which the accommodating party accumulates points for an upcoming situation that is more important. A very different scenario occurs when decisions under this strategy are inspired by altruism and generosity, putting aside other competing ideas and personal interests.

Compromising Strategy

A compromising strategy is a middle-of-the-road strategy between collaborative and competitive behaviors. This strategy is one of the most widely used. Each party imposes something and gives up something until both parties reach an agreement that might not fully satisfy either one, but will not impose undue harm on any of them. A middle-ground solution implies exchanging concessions and splitting benefits and costs between parties so that each participant wins something and loses something. The distribution achieved is considered equitable by both parties, and the agreement is mutually acceptable despite shortcomings in the solution.

The compromising strategy may help negotiate when time is limited, the relationship is occasional, information is scarce and both parties have compelling arguments that don't find significant resistance. This strategy may consolidate the relationship between the parties for future negotiations and avoid risks and breakdowns.

Collaborating Strategy

The collaborating strategy is more demanding than the previous ones. Both cooperative and competitive behaviors are simultaneously present. This form of conflict resolution requires an effort to identify the two parties' underlying interests and find solutions that satisfy them. The aim is to attain mutual benefits for a win-win situation (Fisher, Ury, and Patton, 2011). It may imply exploring disagreements for both parties to learn from their experiences or face interpersonal differences to find creative solutions.

Collaborating is an alternative to the compromising strategy that demands more effort to search for creative and novel forms of stating the matters under negotiation, seeking mutual gains. The process starts when parties express their position and underlying interests, with the intent to identify whether what appears to be conflicting interests can be reconciled, thus creating value for both parties. The parties' collaboration leads to a redefinition of the matter under negotiation, as indicated in the Harvard Method, developed by Fisher and Ury at the Law School. It postulates that negotiations should seek mutual benefits first and foremost. The Harvard Method highlights the legitimacy of a result based on fair criteria, independent of the parties' interests and preferences. The negotiation process should satisfy both parties' legitimate interests, producing long-lasting effects that improve the relationship and avoid damage and deterioration (Fisher, Ury, and Patton, 2011).

Collaboration strategy implies a significant effort from both parties to get to know each other, understand what each one intends to achieve, inquire about their interests, objectives and possible restrictions, and to assess their positions in advance of the negotiation process. It requires patience and intensive research, data analysis and agility to ask relevant questions with the potential to impact the outcome. This effort allows elaborating the best proposal the negotiating parties can make to get a win-win solution.

Win-win negotiation is a process of creating and discovering new alternatives and options to continue the negotiation when an agreement is hard to reach. It requires every possible effort to reach a mutually satisfying agreement through an in-depth exploration of each party's different resources and abilities. These joint and common efforts expand the available benefits for both parties, increasing mutual gains. This strategy creates value before going into the task of fairly distributing the proceeds. The key is to recognize and productively manage tensions between the cooperative and competitive actions to minimize the time needed and avoid demanding excessive effort from people.

Malhotra and Bazerman (2007) define the collaborating strategy as an "investigative negotiation process" to get to know the counterpart's real intentions and objectives. In this negotiation, both parties must avoid rigid positions that obstruct reaching an agreement. Trust and cooperation are of the essence to get a successful collaborative negotiation strategy. They propose five principles of "investigative negotiations":

- Don't' focus on *what* the counterpart requires but on *why* they do so. When understanding what's behind a position, individuals may propose new options and open new perspectives.
- Direct your attention to the counterpart's constraints to understand why they cannot compromise at a certain point. Mitigating restrictions of the other party may help in maintaining a negotiation that might have failed.

- Focus on alternatives mutually convenient for both parties, instead of competing for the benefits.
- Visualize the opportunities that the demands of the counterpart might offer to advance your interests. If this is possible, the agreements will be satisfactory to both parties.
- Don't give up, even if the negotiation seems hopeless. Keep searching for a win-win solution.

The collaborating strategy is undoubtedly the preferred one in long-term dealings. It is used mainly in family relationships and work teams, where there is a community of interests. But it is not always feasible in every setting due to time constraints or other reasons. Other strategies can be more effective, particularly the popular compromising strategy, based on splitting the difference.

Negotiation: The Civilized Way of Dealing with Conflict

An orderly negotiation process, with the active participation of parties involved, is preferable over other conflict resolution forms, such as using force, exercising authority or engaging in legal arbitrations and trials that may be quite expensive. Today relationships are more symmetrical and less hierarchical; hence it becomes more pertinent than ever to develop negotiating abilities to address conflicts and differences.

Entering a negotiation requires considering two factors: style and strategy. Each person brings to the table a *negotiation style* that is the natural or learned predisposition to use a preferred pattern of conflict resolution. The *negotiation strategy* refers to the decision to use one or a blend of conflict resolution strategies depending on circumstances and stage of the negotiation process.

Negotiation Style

The negotiation style refers to the typical approach a person uses to address conflictive situations. This approach is one or a blend of the five strategies previously described: Avoiding, Competing, Accommodating, Compromising and Collaborating.

Thomas and Kilmann (1977) developed a widely used 30-item questionnaire (TKI) to measure negotiation style. Each item forces people to choose between two alternatives, and their preferences show whether they favor cooperative or competitive behavior in conflict resolution.

The *negotiation style profile* is a pattern showing the prevalence (frequency and intensity) with which a person uses each one of the five strategies identified in Table 8.1. This way of measuring the negotiation profile discriminates very well between people, as it identifies various negotiation approaches.[1]

All persons have a way of being that makes them lean towards a relationship style with their counterpart when facing a conflict. The negotiation profile obtained is associated with personality factors and training in these styles, but family upbringing and relationships with friends also impact negotiation style.

The personal negotiation style is a critical variable when entering a negotiation process because a priori, it sets a limit to what a person can do. Therefore, leaders need to know their negotiation style, strengths and improvement areas to plan the negotiation strategy. The idea is to behave naturally and rely on their skills, without pretending to be different.

Negotiation Strategy

The most effective negotiation strategy is contingent on the nature of the conflict and prevailing circumstances. The negotiation strategy involves choosing the best way to deal with the situation.

The first issue is to choose a *negotiation approach*. It refers to the adoption of a way to interact with the counterpart. This approach may be any of the five conflict resolution strategies in Table 8.1, but the selection may change as the negotiation process evolves.

Then comes selecting a person suitable to negotiate. The idea is that this person has a negotiating style that fits the chosen strategy. For instance, it would be inappropriate to use as negotiator a person with a predominant competing style when the best way to deal with the conflict is by using an avoiding strategy.

Moreover, as the negotiation strategy may vary along the process, the preferred style should change too. For instance, at the beginning of the negotiation process it may be better to grant a concession to strengthen personal relationships with the counterpart, addressing the more substantive issues later in the process.

Changes in the negotiation strategy require changes in the negotiation style. It is a flexibility requirement not easy for a single person. That is why it is better to have a negotiating team made up of people with complementary negotiation styles to alternate at critical negotiation moments.

The Negotiation Process

Best practices in negotiation processes have been the subject of study by many authors. One of the best known is the award-winning Harvard method (Fisher, Ury, and Patton, 2011). This negotiation approach seeks an agreement that satisfies both parties' interests and complies with the principles of *distributive justice*. It means that both parties make their best effort to be fair, use legitimate procedures to achieve mutually beneficial results and commit to honor the agreement. In this way, the perception is that the negotiation process is fair, and its outcome must improve or, at least, not deteriorate the relationship between the negotiating parties.

Sebenius (2001) provides a blueprint of the Harvard Method when referring to the "six habits of effective negotiators".

1. *Try to perceive the problem from the perspective of the counterpart.* Solving the counterpart's problem may be the best way to address the situation. "Put yourself in the shoes of the other party" to gather information about the central points of the negotiation, understand the interests and motivations of the counterpart, and to establish a climate of trust.
2. *Price is certainly important, but that's not all that matters.* The economic assessment cannot be the only indicator used to evaluate the outcome of the negotiation process. It also matters how to achieve the result, leading to a trust relationship that may end a long-standing conflict between the parties or open new future opportunities.
3. *Look after the* common interest *and beware of* unyielding positions. What is essential is to understand how the deal affects interests and not to adopt positions that make it more difficult to reach agreements. In these cases, unyielding positions are harmful to everyone. Instead of a win-win solution, the outcome is a lose-lose situation.
4. *Consensus does not necessarily lead to the best agreement.* The consensus is not an end per se. It is a desirable situation, not an imperative. Reaching an early consensus can signal a less efficient agreement for the parties. Differences may become opportunities for creative solutions.
5. *The agreement reached must be better than the alternative of withdrawing from the negotiation.* The negotiation outcome must comply with a basic rule: Each of the parties in the agreement must improve its situation. Otherwise, it is preferable to go for the Best Alternative to a Negotiated Agreement (BATNA).
6. *A useful reminder: Never forget biases.* Personal biases are a barrier when negotiating. People unavoidably interpret information favoring their interests and positions (complacency bias), overestimate the correctness of their vision (partisan perception) and fall into the trap of *group thinking* (adhering to group opinion without proper scrutiny). Therefore, it is good to have an external *benchmark*, such as the participation of people who do not belong to the organization.

Preparing the Negotiation

Negotiation involves persuasion, which requires significant preparation, gathering information, expert knowledge and practical training. The outcome of many negotiations depends on the effort before the process. Most negotiations are won or lost in advance before the discussion begins due to the prior preparation quality. Preparation effectiveness depends on the degree of complexity and difficulty of the negotiation.

Commonly, negotiations occur in a context of confusion, uncertainty and doubts about the parties' intentions, which often makes them hard to understand and to monitor. All leaders confront these uncertainty levels as do the people closely related to the negotiation process, making the need for preparation still more pressing.

Some Negotiating Tactics

There are plenty of books suggesting different tips to approach negotiations. Based on Saieh, Rodríguez and Opazo (2006), the following ideas include valuable recommendations.

- *Identify effective communication channels in advance.* It is a critical condition for a successful negotiation. The idea is to rely on one main or "official channel" and, if possible, other parallel channels to convey messages to different counterparts. It may be challenging, but it is often useful to unlock complicated negotiation processes.
- *Know your counterpart.* Knowledge about the other party's principles, actions and behaviors allows monitoring and adjusting the negotiation's rhythms. Managing the timing and the rhythm of a negotiation process is a central issue that requires a unique sensibility and perceptions of people and events as they develop. It means, among other things, realizing when to get strict with norms and when to concede, making sure to avoid confrontations. Without a conscious effort of all parties, a disagreement may spark a spiral of hostilities.
- *Use humor.* A sense of humor may be a helpful tool to deal with conflicts constructively. Adequate and timely humor may help avoid an impasse, releasing tensions of the participants, alleviating difficult moments. It is a useful negotiation tactic.
- *Use of words and silences.* Negotiation experts excel at delivering and retaining information and managing rhythms, deadlines, symbols, gestures and implicit messages. They can interpret how, what and why the other party communicates through a large variety of expressions. They are familiar with criteria for generating and evaluating options, establishing explicit norms and skillfully persuading the counterpart.
- *Anchor the negotiation on a good starting point.* Effective collaborative negotiations need a good starting point because introducing changes in offerings and concessions during the negotiation process make reaching an agreement more difficult. The starting point in a negotiation is identifying the problem or conflict, circumscribing main issues to a few relevant topics, and reducing the conversations' complexity.

- *Generate a vast number of options.* This facilitates selecting some of them and reaching an agreement. Do not stick to positions with the potential to put a cooperation agreement at risk. Avoid intimidation by the other party's obstinacy leading to outcomes where one party wins all while the other loses. This result is opposite to the win-win negotiation strategy.
- *Get a partner.* Getting the right negotiation partner, familiar with the subject in conflict, can make a significant difference.
- *Find alliances.* Find alliances with the potential to increase the value generated in the negotiation process.
- *Exchange of information.* The collaborating strategy also needs to stress deals with the other party to increase mutual understanding of interests and clarify positions.
- *Make sure you have a BATNA.*[2] Having an alternative if the negotiation stalls and there is no agreement provides confidence to accept or reject options under consideration.
- *Active listening.* It is undoubtedly helpful to listen actively, with sympathy, assuming the counterpart's point of view; however, when the process affects the parties' interests, they will naturally react, asserting differences.
- *Manage emotions, separating people from the negotiation problem.* Emotions are a natural and critical human response to favorable or adverse circumstances and, consequently, central to negotiation processes. Thus, it is essential to create an atmosphere of trust and mutual respect required to manage emotions effectively, creating a positive and transparent environment, and maintaining consistency between saying and acting.
- *Avoid early competitive closures.* Keep away from derailing the negotiation with early competitive closures that can prevent agreements and mutual commitments.
- *The use of power is out in a win-win negotiation.* Using imposition requires deep consideration and intense assessment because it is opposite to collaborative negotiation approaches, and it does not fit a Sensible Leadership.
- *Intercultural negotiations.* International negotiations require negotiators with different knowledge and skills because the preparation and the process demand special attention to details that cannot be overlooked and are ignored or taken for granted in the negotiators' national or cultural origin. Each culture has unique characteristics and peculiarities that make it difficult to interpret and decipher what is considered appropriate behavior. It can lead to significant disruptions in the relationship between parties, ignoring sensibilities with unintentional harm.

Notes

1 The results of this instrument's application, presented on a percentile table, show the five negotiating strategies' frequency of use in a person's repertoire. These results are benchmarked against standardized scores to interpret how common or infrequent is the person's profile in terms of using different strategies for conflict resolution.
2 BATNA: Best alternative to a negotiated agreement

References

Abarca, N. (2017). *Intelligent Negotiation (Negociación inteligente)*. Santiago, Chile: Ediciones El Mercurio.

Fisher, R., Ury, W., and Patton, B (2011). *Getting to Yes: Negotiating Agreement Without Giving In*, 3rd Ed. New York, NY: Penguin Books.

Kimberlyn, L., Pillemer, J., and Wheeler, M. (2013). Negotiating with emotion. *Harvard Business Review*, January-February, 96–103.

Malhotra, D., and Bazerman, M. H. (2007). Investigative negotiation, *Harvard Business Review*, September, 73–78.

Morrow, L. (1985). Behind closed doors, *Time*, December 2, p. 17.

Pondy, L. R. (1967). Organizational conflict: concepts and models. *Administrative Science Quarterly*, 12(2), 296–320. Retrieved: http://dx.doi.org/10.2307/2391553

Saieh, C., Rodríguez, D., and Opazo, M. P. (2006). *Negotiation: Collaboration or Competition? (Negociación: ¿Cooperar o competir?)*. Santiago, Chile: El Mercurio Aguilar.

Sebenius, J. (2001). Six habits of merely effective negotiators. *Harvard Business Review*, April, 87–95.

Thomas, K. (1992). Conflict and conflict management: reflections and update. *Journal of Organizational Behavior*, 13, 265–274.

Thomas, K., and Kilmann, R. (1977). Developing a forced-choice measure of conflict behavior: the "MODE" Instrument. *Educational and Psychological Measurement*, 37, 309–325.

Part III

The Sensible Leader

Sensible Leadership stems from the theories and practices of Human Centered Management (Lepeley, 2017). The continuous improvement of followers' wellbeing is essential for organizations to attain long-term sustainability (Ochoa, Lepeley, and Essens, 2019). Human and social relationships are at the heart of Sensible Leadership.

The sensible leader acts with insight and prudence in three settings: the relationship with followers, the political forces present in the organization, and the social dimension of management. They refer to the individual, organizational and societal levels in which leaders act.

In the relationship with followers, insight refers to the leader's ability to perceive and interpret coworkers' feelings, emotions, how they generate expectations and shape opinions and perceptions. Prudence appears in the leaders' Emotional Intelligence to act thoughtfully in each event. Insight and prudence in the relationship with followers is the subject of Chapter 9.

When dealing with the organization's political forces, insight refers to the leader's ability to perceive the objectives and interests of the various groups competing to impose their views on the organization. Prudence shows in leaders' efforts to properly manage decision-making, reach a negotiated solution and exercise power sensibly. Insight and prudence, when dealing with the political forces in the organization, is the subject of Chapter 10.

Finally, management's social dimension requires insight to perceive changes and trends in the environment and the implications for coworkers' and stakeholders' wellbeing. Prudence appears in the decision-making of leaders adjusted to societal trends and the human needs of stakeholders. The social dimension of management is the subject of Chapter 11.

Moreover, sensible leaders are integral persons; this means that they perform rightly in the personal and work environments. The *integral sensible leader* is the subject of Chapter 12.

The book closes with Chapter 13, which links Sensible Leadership with *ethical leadership*.

References

Lepeley, M.T. (2017). *Human Centered Management. The 5 Pillars of Organizational Quality and Global Sustainability.* Routledge.
Ochoa, P., Lepeley, M.T., and Essens, P. (2019). *Wellbeing for Sustainability in the Global Workplace.* Routledge.

9 Relationship with Followers

Sensible Leadership gives high priority to the relationship with followers. Leaders as individuals receive much attention in leadership studies, but they need followers; otherwise, leadership is meaningless. There are no leaders without followers willing to go along with them, take the risk of trusting them, be part of their projects and dreams, and become jointly responsible for advancing the organizational mission. Leaders need followers, just as followers need leaders. Grint (2005) pointed out that "It only takes followers to do nothing for leadership to fail". Coworkers are indeed followers when they recognize and accept the influence of leaders.

The quality of the relationship with followers is critical in workplace wellbeing, engagement and organizational sustainability. Leaders must strive to be in tune with their followers and delicately manage their relationships. They must be open to the proposals of followers and, should a disagreement arise, act with determination and settle differences fairly, to avoid conflicts.

Good management of the relationship with followers requires Emotional Intelligence (EI). The measurement of Emotional Intelligence is Emotional Quotient (EQ). Sensible leaders have a high EQ. Although knowledge and hard skills are necessary to reach a leadership position, leadership sustainability depends mostly on Emotional Intelligence and Soft Skills (Lepeley, Beutell, Abarca, and Majluf, 2021).

Sensible leaders know how to manage their own emotions, understand their followers' feelings and motivations and express emotions aligned with specific situations. Leaders' EI allows them to assume job responsibility, staying tuned with followers to manage productive and fulfilling relationships. They are open to discuss new ideas and innovative proposals of collaborators and they establish respectful and empathetic relationships with them.

Emotional Intelligence

Daniel Goleman (2004), a psychologist who pioneered EI, defined it in terms of "personal characteristics" and "interactions with others". The *personal characteristics* of EI include *self-knowledge, self-management* and *self-motivation.*

Personal Characteristics

Self-knowledge: Openness and Authenticity

Individuals with high EQ are aware of their inner world, state of mind and feelings. A high EQ means knowing what is right and wrong with them, their qualities and shortcomings, preferences and what they want and don't want. In sum, they are self-confident and accept the way they are, with their strengths and limitations; and they are clear about their emotions, so they feel assured about their abilities and how they live their lives.

Sensible leaders with EI are *open individuals* who don't judge, censure or isolate themselves. They pay attention, without trying to control the situation, impose their views or stand as a judge of others' behavior.

Also, sensible leaders are *authentic individuals* who behave in the same way in private and public settings, with coworkers and family and friends. Authenticity is a quality that others see and ascribe to a person. An individual *is not* authentic but *is perceived* by others as authentic when they show prudent behavior and deference to understand other people.

Authenticity is an attribute people acquire with sensitivity and experience that requires control and prudence in behavior. It is not synonymous with unrestricted *openness.* Sensible leaders realize that what may be a great attribute in some circles may be a source of countless difficulties in other cases. For instance, being witty may be fun at a party, but it can be very inappropriate in a serious meeting. But this same sense of humor in a conflictive situation can be handy to solve the problem. That is why authenticity requires capturing the atmosphere and understanding the moment's complexity so that leaders' influence is exercised simultaneously with transparency and delicacy.

Authentic leaders adjust their behavior to the context without losing their originality. The balance between conformity and uniqueness, which requires self-knowledge and deciding what to reveal about oneself, is very delicate.

Self-management: Measured Behavior

Sensible leaders understand and manage their emotions, take time for reflection, and behave with prudence and integrity. Like all human beings, they have impulses, but they know how to manage emotions and moods, to maintain equanimity under stress and remain calm and confident in crises.

Sensible leaders have the ability, skills and willpower to control their actions and effectively manage complex situations of fast-paced decisions. They create a space of reflection and an atmosphere of confidence while immersed in the middle of pressures to act. They focus their attention on more relevant and lasting achievements, avoiding being distracted by short-term retributions. The measured behavior of leaders is not only a personal virtue but a strength of sustainable organizations.

Self-motivation

Sensible leaders are self-motivated, exhibit *achievement motivation* and spare no effort to accomplish personal and team goals and objectives to increase performance and productivity for long-term sustainability. They seek opportunities to innovate and continuously improve and respond with promptness and excellence. The search for quality standards is the hallmark of their purpose and actions.

Sensible leaders take pride in organizational achievements but assume their responsibility entirely. They admit their faults and deal with problems without becoming obsessed with failure. They show optimism and a sense of humor, having a high capacity to laugh at themselves and their mistakes, persisting in their efforts despite obstacles and setbacks in the local and global VUCA (volatile, uncertain, complex, ambiguous) environment.

Interactions with Others

The "interactions with others" of EI involves *empathy* and *social talent*.

Empathy

Empathy is the ability to recognize emotions and feelings in the interactions with other people, to stand in their place and correctly interpret their moods and motivations. Sensible leaders are distinguishable by their unequivocal demonstrations of empathy.

Empathic leaders adjust their behavior to the circumstances before reacting, providing a warm and objective response, without falling into a compassionate attitude that may impair the situation. *Empathic concern* refers to the willingness and ability to perceive the support the other person needs.

Empathy has a *cognitive dimension* and an *emotional dimension*. The cognitive dimension is the ability to look at situations from the perspective of another person. The emotional one is the ability to experience someone else's feelings to connect with the emotions reflected in their face, voice and other subtle nonverbal signs that reveal sentiments. Sensible leaders show tact and consideration for others.

Social Talent: Managing Relationships

Sensible leaders excel at *social talent*, which is an essential capability of Emotional Intelligence. It is the art of relating to other people, managing emotions and acting with empathy. They manifest feelings and behave prudently, in tune with the specific situation.

Relationships with others must adjust to the social context. For instance, there are differences in how to relate to senior people, family or close friends. Similarly, the rules of behavior change when moving from the workplace to a party. There is an implicit code of conduct in *good manners*.

Sensible leaders excel in social talents. They have a broad network, build teams, generate agreements and motivate people to participate in a collaborative project.

Social talent is key to the sensible leaders' performance and ability to drive change and innovation because teamwork and networking are essential in Human Centered Organizations.

Sensible leaders listen with openness, are skilled communicators and send compelling messages to motivate followers and stimulate their abilities. As a result, they promote an open and creative work environment where talents and teamwork flourish. They also encourage diversity, seeking a balance between collaboration and competition to achieve common goals. And in case conflictive or difficult situations arise, they favor win-win negotiations over forcing a decision.

Socially talented leaders build lasting and trustworthy ties among people, fostering all previous Emotional Intelligence skills of self-knowledge, moderate behavior and empathy.

Social talent includes *components related to the individual* and *components related to interpersonal relations*.

COMPONENTS RELATED TO THE INDIVIDUAL

The components related to the individual are *assertiveness*, *self-confidence* and *emotional stability*.

Assertiveness Being assertive is about being frank and direct in expressing demands, opinions, feelings and attitudes ("Can you help me with a problem I have?") instead of being evasive ("Are you busy?"). It's very different from being aggressive or passive. Aggressive people present their demands in an insistent, unpleasant and inconsiderate manner. Passive people suppress their ideas, attitudes, feelings and thoughts as if they were afraid others were to oppose them.

Practicing assertiveness means defending your own positions in cases like:

- *Making demands.* Assertive leaders do not hesitate to point out the mistakes made by their collaborators, to demand better performance and to set high expectations. It helps to complete tasks and achieve goals. A non-assertive person usually conforms to the will of others.

- *Expressing desires.* People who express their preferences are often surprised at the results, for instance, considering purchasing an off-budget item and saying, "I like this product, but all I can afford is $750, which is less than the price you ask, can we do business?"
- *Expressing positive feelings.* For instance, telling a coworker, "I'm glad we're participating in this project because I like the way you work".

For most people, it is easier to make demands than to express wishes or positive feelings. Still, assertiveness cannot just be about requests.

Self-confidence   Self-confidence refers to a view of personal abilities and skills that allow positive coping with diverse life circumstances. It is not only a personality trait but a form of behavior appropriate to a wide variety of situations. It will enable staying calm under pressure and keeping composure during a crisis.

Being confident makes it easier to be assertive and get people to improve performance and achieve ambitious goals. For instance, saying, "I know the extreme weather shut us down for four days, but we can make up for lost time if we all cooperate and work smartly. In 30 days, we will have met or exceeded our goals for the quarter."

Developing self-confidence is an ongoing process that refines with each new experience. But it's not enough to have confidence in oneself but to project that confidence to other people.

Self-confident leaders are reliable individuals who inspire self-assurance in their collaborators, mainly because their actions transmit security. Their achievements are congruent with their promises, and they are gentle when communicating accomplishments.

Emotional Stability   Emotional stability refers to the ability to control the emotions that inevitably arise in any relationship. It is an essential trait of leaders because group members always expect to be treated with care. Emotional outbursts can damage the relationship.

Emotional stability is hard to develop, so people who cannot adequately control their emotions should seek professional support to mitigate this weakness.

COMPONENTS RELATED TO INTERPERSONAL RELATIONS

The components related to interpersonal relationships are *being warm and expressive, creating a certain intimacy by sharing real-life stories,* and *using humor.*

Being Warm and Expressive   Being warm and expressive is undoubtedly relevant, but leaders must make sure that collaborators perceive it that way. The fundamental requirement is that these expressions are genuine signs of affection that reflect frankly and with total transparency the moment's feeling, as when telling a loved one, "I am happy to have you with me".

When communicating feelings with subtle gestures, nonverbal emotional expressions are significant. Followers may better perceive a smile, a warm gesture or a good hug of congratulation since they convey that the leader cares and can be trusted.

Creating a Certain Intimacy by Sharing Real-life Stories   When leaders share personal life anecdotes or tell uplifting stories that convey a message, they create an atmosphere of intimacy that encourages many to contribute to the *magic moment* by revealing a chapter of their life. It builds stronger bonds, thus strengthening a relationship of friendship, trust and affection.

Using a Sense of Humor   The appropriate use of humor is perhaps the most effective way to relieve tension, reduce hostility and mitigate monotony in the workplace, thus avoiding the conflicts that are irremediably present in relationships between people. Humor can positively affect the performance of a group of people.

In addition to using humor to smooth things over in periods of tension, the preferred form of comedians and organizational leaders is laughing at themselves when they seem too stern. When mockery is about oneself, no one can feel insulted or undermined.

Emotions in Leadership

Sensible leaders show their EI by applying Soft Skills to capture the attention of followers and awaken their emotions. They excel at the art of sending emotional signals, making them effective communicators. They establish with their followers a personalized relation grounded on emotions, listen to them carefully and recognize their needs and aspirations. They also have a fair evaluation of their skills and potential for development, opening new appropriate opportunities for relevant training and learning from work experience.

This unique relationship of trust makes sensible leaders give followers autonomy, delegate responsibilities and open opportunities to participate in information and decisions. Thus, followers are motivated with the organizational mission, gaining their support and commitment.

Emotions are fundamental for effective leadership and success. Well-managed emotions bring wellbeing to people, leading to high performance, productivity and long-term sustainability. They are present in all the activities of a sensible leader, such as:

Managing the Organizational Culture

Culture is what gives an organization its identity. Members of an organization find meaning in the culture. Culture appears in shared ideologies, values, norms and beliefs, all having significant emotional components.

A Human Centered Organizational Culture (Lepeley, Morales, Essens, Beutell, and Majluf, 2021) shares and promotes positive emotions, articulating them in enticing ways. Handling emotions requires the effective use of Soft Skills (Lepeley, Beutell, Abarca, and Majluf, 2021) as essential elements to secure people's wellbeing in the organization.

Managing the organizational culture is, in some measure, equivalent to the handling of emotions. The need to adhere and identify with culture comes more from emotional needs than from a rational or instrumental perspective. Culture provides members of an organization with socially acceptable ways to express emotions. Going against the norms and values in culture causes a strong adverse reaction.

Generating Self-confidence, Security and Optimism

Leaders with high Emotional Intelligence know the emotions of followers and anticipate their reactions in different circumstances. They can sense true feelings, even if they make efforts to hide them and capably distinguish genuine from simulated emotions.

Leaders' challenge is to manage followers' emotions subtly and encourage them to freely express what they feel and avoid any ill feelings and resentment that may harm communications and attaining common organizational goals. Followers don't have to pretend to have emotions they don't have. In this way, confidence grows in followers. They can confront the problems they face without anxiety, making them appreciate the real value of their knowledge and skills and feel proud of their contribution.

Communicating Shared Organizational Mission in an Engaging Way

Sensible leaders need to get the entire organization to share the mission and collectively work to attain objectives and goals. Communication is essential to vitalize organizational culture and long-term sustainability.

The best way to get followers' attention, mobilize them and open them to the leaders' proposals is to appeal to their emotions and foster a sustainable workplace culture.

Fostering Change and Innovation

To carry out a successful transformation, sensible leaders prepare followers to overcome their natural opposition to risks involved in changes to the status quo. They need to perceive their followers' emotions to surmount their resistance to change, enabling organizational development.

Transformation consolidates when long-term sustainability prevails over short-term comfort with the status quo.

Information Processing

Leaders must identify challenges, threats and opportunities the organization faces in highly uncertain environments. In this endeavor, information and corporate knowledge are usually intricate and convoluted.

Sensible leaders have better processing of the available knowledge. They work with data that are objectively available jointly with information that shows up in their coworkers' emotional states. They are highly perceptive of the moods and sentiments of followers. For instance, if there is an excellent mood in the group, it increases creativity and allows the emergence of a more attractive organizational vision.

Decision-making

When leaders know and manage their own emotions, they can use them to improve their decisions. Jointly with Emotional Intelligence comes agile thinking, making connections between apparently unrelated information, recognizing associations among issues and considering different scenarios to avoid decision-making rigidity.

The clues emotions provide on a given issue help prioritize multiple demands leaders face, helping them focus on events that need prompt consideration, like opportunities and risks that call for immediate attention. Also, sensible leaders need to manage negative emotions to avoid interference with decision-making.

The Social Intelligence Model

Social intelligence (Boyatzis and Goleman, 2008) is an extension of Emotional Intelligence based on the emerging field of social neuroscience. The research shows that the actions and emotions of one person directly impact another person. Due to the existence of *mirror neurons*, a person copies feelings and behaviors like laughter, grief, restlessness, and movements and gestures that may indicate approval or disapproval, bringing in the sense of shared experience.

Sensible leaders acknowledge the importance of attending to the needs, fears and concerns of followers. But they also must solve pressing problems and make critical decisions to sustain the business. These two activities trigger different parts of the brain. Sensible leaders can privilege either the brain network that enables task-focused attention needed to solve problems, or the one that facilitates reflection, compassion and social connection. They need to form and confirm their thoughts and be open to followers' opinions, perspectives and feelings. According to Melvin Smith, Ellen Van Oosten, and Richard E. Boyatzis (2020), "the most effective leaders do indeed use both, and they can toggle back and forth between them in a fraction of a second". They excel in Emotional Intelligence.

Sensible leaders use their Emotional Intelligence to tune in to followers' genetic copying behaviors to influence them in positive ways, including being generous with smiling and using other empathetic signals such as hugs, greetings, handshakes and comments about a good job. This social *resonance* between people occurs in a fraction of a second, intuitively, due to the human brain's characteristics, but has the potential of long-lasting results.

While people interact, what happens in the brain reveals that sensible leaders are aware of the impact of their followers' behavior and respond accordingly. Therefore, what matters is "to develop the talent and genuine interest to generate positive feelings in the people the leader seeks to attract to get their cooperation and support" (Boyatzis and Goleman, 2008). The way to communicate the message is more important than its content.

Leaders Need To Be Aware of their Limitations

Sensible leaders are aware of the limitations of their capacities and the insufficiency of their actions. MIT professors call this an *incomplete leader* (Ancona, Malone, Orlikowski, and Senge, 2007).

Sensible leaders recognize their shortcomings and accept their responsibility when wrong but aspire to do their best and seek people's wellbeing. When they don't get it, they admit their mistakes, ask for understanding and make every effort to overcome difficulties.

Therefore, when saying that good leaders have *Emotional Intelligence* or *social intelligence*, we must understand that they are doing their best to meet high demands. Their commitment to doing things right is so evident that followers will look benevolently at their limitations and support them to move forward. Followers feel affection and respect for their leaders. They know they are working for all people in the organization, and not for personal benefits.

Leaders don't have to be perfect to be effective: they can be *incomplete*. They cannot be required to have all the skills to a superlative degree. It is enough for them to know the organization's people who can help them overcome their limitations. Leadership is not about doing things alone but working with those who can help them address their abilities or knowledge gaps.

Organizations are collective efforts that rest on the collaborative work of many people at all levels. Today, in the age of knowledge, there is a need to have followers who are experts in their fields and make contributions that no one else can make. Sensible leaders are not shy about asking the participation of expert people who complement their knowledge in the areas they have not mastered and integrate the many followers who contribute to implementing every organizational initiative. Leaders don't have to be geniuses, but they must know when and how to ask expert people for the help they need to get their support and commitment.

Indeed, leaders need to be self-confident and not feel diminished by people's help, even when coming from lower hierarchical levels. And although it may seem paradoxical, acting this way makes them closer and highly regarded, because followers recognize the humility and fortitude to ask for the needed help. On the contrary, if they show the fear of appearing vulnerable, their behavior ends up harming them and the entire organization.

References

Ancona, D., Malone, T. W, Orlikowski, W. J., and Senge, P. M. (2007). In praise of the incomplete leader. *Harvard Business Review*, February, 92–100.

Boyatzis, R., and Goleman, D. (2008). Social intelligence and the biology of leadership. *Harvard Business Review*, September, 74–81.

Goleman, D. (2004). What makes a leader. *Harvard Business Review*, January, 82–91.

Grint, K. (2005). *Leadership: Limits and Possibilities*. New York, NY: Palgrave MacMillan.

Lepeley, M. T., Beutell, N., Abarca, N., Majluf, N. (eds.). (2021). *Soft Skills for Human Centered Management and Global Sustainability*, Routledge.

Lepeley, M. T., Morales, O., Essens, P., Beutell, N., and Majluf, N., (eds.). (2021). *Human Centered Organizational Culture: Global Dimensions*. Routledge.

Smith, M., Van Oosten, E., Boyatzis, R. E. (2020). The best managers balance analytical and emotional intelligence. *Harvard Business Review*, June.

10 Political Forces at Work in the Organization

Sensible leaders cultivate their political sensibility and participate with delicacy in power relations. They know that power is an unavoidable component of the organizational landscape and that decision-making is a political and negotiation process (Allison and Zelikow, 1999).

Sensible leaders need a deep understanding of organizational life and a clear comprehension of the political consequences of their actions and decisions. They must anticipate their impact on external and internal stakeholders and over people and groups that are either benefited or harmed, adapting their behavior accordingly.

Decisions made in an organization are not just decrees that arise from a rational calculation of benefits and costs, but the consequence of a political process that confronts various contending groups trying to impose their points of view. Sensible leaders are true masters in cultivating strong relationships with people both outside and inside the organization to get the help of allies or neutralize opponents in difficult political decisions. Their actions and points of view can affect the interests of the organization, directly or indirectly, either to improve or to deteriorate the wellbeing of people. It is no wonder that this network of relations is a *personal capital* of leaders and a real *social capital* of the organization that can generate significant benefits.

Sensible leaders use *subtle power*, always looking for the best way to influence followers without forcing them and promoting wellbeing and the common good. Thinking that leading is to *give orders* is very harmful, since it ignores the diligent work of the whole organization and disrupts the formal decision-making process. Sensible leaders set limits to their power (Porter, Lorsch, and Nohria, 2004).

Decisions as a Political Process

Politics is at the core of every organization. Leaders have to deal with people who think differently and do not share the same interests. They must seek agreements and promote collaboration to move forward and carry out the shared vision without giving away individual or group benefits.

Every human organization has a political component and must be open to compromise and negotiation, which is an integral part of relationships in a political context. Direct or indirect influence and persuasion are at the core of political processes for negotiating conflicting positions, of either individuals or groups.

The various coalitions or interest groups confront their views in a political negotiation process to move forward their positions and obtain resources. They have to convince their counterpart of their idea's advantages, highlighting its virtues and lessening its shortcomings. Sensible leaders know how to handle the conflicting interests at a rational level and properly manage emotions.

In this process, they strive to get help for the ideas they favor and counterbalance individuals who oppose them, always looking at the organization's overall good and not of specific individuals or groups. This political handling of the situation is necessary to engage a broad coalition to support the project, enlist the main actors and overcome resistance. Table 10.1 provides a blueprint of the typical steps of a political process (Hamel, 2000).

Decisions as a Negotiation Process

At the heart of a political process lies inevitably a negotiation process. When leaders force their views on followers, they are going to find high resistance and generate hard-to-solve conflicts.

Sensible leaders act very differently. They are willing to negotiate, exchange points of view, give liberally to get something back in return. That is why negotiation is an essential part of leadership. It is the civilized way of dealing with divergence and conflict, to make them a source of learning and growth, and not a trap that destroys individuals and organizations.

Negotiation processes are right when maintaining a relationship of mutual respect and appreciation between the parties. As a result, a fair negotiation process opens the door for new future agreements. Parties must care for their relationship with all people participating in the negotiation and those affected by the result.

Individuals who negotiate are in a very demanding situation. They should certainly be concerned with achieving a good result, but not at their counterpart's expense. Both are part of organizations that impose significant restrictions on their freedom to take risks but have full accountability. It is one of those numerous cases where the responsibility far exceeds the authority. The future of individuals in the organization may depend on the negotiation outcome, even if they cannot control all intervening factors. Therefore, sensible negotiators will always leave an honorable exit to the other party and explain the agreements to all interested parties.

Table 10.1 Steps in a Political Process

Step 1: Build a point of view	Imagine a project that is credible (based on objective and verifiable data), coherent (proposed ideas point in the same direction), compelling (exciting, worth the effort) and, in the case of a business firm, with commercial value, based on a recognized competitive advantage and making a clear value proposition to customers.
Step 2: Write a manifesto	Disseminate the project in a way that captures people's imagination, in order to *infect* the organization. Propose a hopeful and forward-looking project.
Step 3: Create a coalition	Form a work team that is committed to the project. Recruit people who contribute without being impatient. Go step by step to get new members.
Step 4: Pick your targets and moments	Acting at the right time often means waiting, postponing the decision, not making unnecessary policy definitions, defining the order of matters in the agenda and managing deadlines with flexibility. But acting decisively when the right moment arrives.
Step 5: Co-opt and neutralize	Make win-win proposals that will also benefit those who resist the project, in order to enlarge the coalition. Become a facilitator rather than a competitor.
Step 6: Find a translator	Find someone who communicates the project with conviction and interest, as a good story, drawing on a diversity of experiences and values, and using all kinds of speeches to get the message across to people.
Step 7: Win small, win early, win often	The best argument for a project is success. Move from idea to action as soon as possible. Make people feel the project as real, even if implementation is still under way. An early achievement, however small, is valuable. Many small achievements throughout the implementation process keep the interest of leaders and the enthusiasm of participants alive. Watch out with promises that can't be delivered.
Step 8: Isolate the project, infiltrate the organization and integrate	To give a project of change in an organization a real chance of success, it is necessary to isolate or protect it at the beginning, in order to prevent bureaucracy from crushing it. Then, to integrate it in the normal activities of the organization, a careful plan of infiltration must be devised.

In a negotiation process, all gestures are relevant, such as the formality of meetings, conversation protocols and interpersonal interactions. All forms of exchange between the parties carry symbolic meaning. Many nonverbal signs have great significance, like the flow of empathy and trust established between the parties. Also meaningful are the glances, the handling of emotions and the management of rhythms and negotiation times. The simultaneous use of rigidity and cession, and toughness and understanding are signs of a well-managed process.

Finally, an unavoidable consequence of negotiation processes is the ethical dimension derived from the negotiation outcome and how to carry the process. The agreement and the way to get it are both crucial. The impact on the lives of negotiators and people affected by the results is inevitable.

References

Allison, G. T., and Zelikow, P. (1999). *Essence of Decision: Explaining the Cuban Missile Crisis*, New York: Longman.

Hamel, G. (2000). *Leading the Revolution*. Boston, MA: Harvard Business School Press.

Porter, M., Lorsch, J., and Nohria, N. (2004). Seven surprises for new CEOs. *Harvard Business Review*, October, 62–72.

11 Social Dimension of Management

The new economic, social and cultural tensions demand that leaders find a new way to exercise their leadership in all areas of activity and not restricted to the organization's inner limits. It is challenging to be a leader today, in a world that has seen radical changes in various areas of life. Leaders are often described as *architects of vision*, who understand their organization's context, read the trends and identify opportunities and risks. They detect in advance the patterns in the environment, before they are evident, and implement timely changes. It is a forceful and practical expression of a *strategic vision* that defines a blueprint for the organization to respond to the *signs of the times*.

Sensible leaders pay special attention to the organizational social context. They consider corporate social responsibility as a personal mission. They focus on the wellbeing of people inside and outside the organization, attending to critical stakeholders' needs; among them, customers, employees, suppliers, community and shareholders. The concern for people is a central issue.

The focus on stakeholders has been clearly behind the influential 2019 "Redefinition of the Purpose of a Corporation" of the Business Roundtable and the 2020 "Davos Manifesto" of the World Economic Forum.[1] Their proposals call for a new business model that will contribute to stakeholders and society's wellbeing and achieve economic profitability.

The Business Roundtable commitment to stakeholders of August 19, 2019 focuses on the responsibility business firms should assume in their relations with stakeholders:

- Delivering value to our customers. We will further the tradition of American companies leading the way in meeting or exceeding customer expectations.
- Investing in our employees. It starts with compensating them fairly and providing essential benefits. It also includes supporting them through training and education to develop new skills for a rapidly changing world. We foster diversity and inclusion, dignity, and respect.

- Dealing fairly and ethically with our suppliers. We serve as partners to the other companies, large and small, that help us meet our missions.
- Supporting the communities in which we work. We respect the people in our communities and protect the environment by embracing sustainable practices across our businesses.
- Generating long-term value for shareholders who provide the capital allowing companies to invest, grow, and innovate. We are committed to transparency and active engagement with shareholders.

The 2020 Davos Manifesto is also very telling (Schwab, 2019):

- Stakeholders' capitalism rests on private corporations as trustees of the society.
- A corporation is not just a profit-seeking entity but also a social organism.
- A purely profit-seeking behavior caused shareholder capitalism to become increasingly disconnected from the real economy.
- The "Davos Manifesto" describes a firm's principal responsibilities toward its stakeholders.
- Companies should pay their fair share of taxes, show zero tolerance for corruption, uphold human rights throughout their global supply chains, and advocate for a competitive level playing field – particularly in the "platform economy".
- All companies should work with other stakeholders to improve the state of the world they are operating. It should be their ultimate purpose. "Shared value creation" includes "environmental, social, and governance" (ESG) goals as a complement to standard financial metrics.

Human Centered Organizations try to meet the economic, social and environmental expectations of all stakeholders. Sensible leaders establish equitable relations with all of them. Their perception of being fairly treated by the company is essential. The ethics code reveals the firm's commitment to building relationships focused on the wellbeing of stakeholders. The contents of a typical ethics code are discussed in the remainder of this chapter (Majluf, 2021).

Relationships with Employees

Human Centered Organizations provide *quality jobs* that meet employees' material and spiritual needs. Simultaneously, they contribute to the company's progress.

Just offering job opportunities is not enough. There are many characteristics of quality jobs. The pillars of the relationship between the employee and the organization are *fair wages* and a *shared project* that gives meaning to work. Other relevant management concerns are fostering interpersonal relationships, promoting diversity and inclusion, barring all forms of discrimination, sharing information openly, building trust and handling conflicts as learning opportunities. Other important issues are the respect for personal interests and spaces of intimacy with friends and family, and the concern for occupational health and safety that require the company to control work risks and offer comfortable and attractive areas to operate.

Quality jobs also provide an *engaging work environment* built on mutual care and respect and with a focus on employees' wellbeing. To get people's engagement, they must have a sense of achievement and feel that their work is worthwhile. They must appreciate the result of their effort and be proud of what they do. Issues such as product quality, customer satisfaction and innovation are all relevant matters.

Opening spaces for participation in information and decisions and giving employees autonomy and responsibility is central in designing jobs that offer opportunities to develop people's creative, professional and human potential. Often, leaders are described as *Architects of Social Spaces* when promoting their followers' autonomous behavior. For that, they create social spaces and define the constitution that regulates interpersonal relationships and act as "entrepreneurs of meaning" (Hamel, 2009). Leaders set the rules and give their followers ample space to assume their responsibility, develop their talents and create their future (Senge, 2004). They don't rule with an iron fist. In this way, they establish the conditions that increase the *social capital* of the organization. It is critical in its performance because organizations are collaborative efforts of many people. It is crucial to strengthen interpersonal relationships to build bridges that generate closeness, solve conflicts and awaken creativity. Simple solutions facilitate creating social links, like having a coffee room for people to meet and talk about trivia or address topics of high relevance. A curious alternative is to have *meetings to do nothing*, where people meet informally with no work scheduled. These are spaces where the best of human beings flourish since their humanity arises when having a positive and deep relationship with other people.

Relationships with Customers

The organization focuses on meeting or exceeding customer expectations, delivering excellent products and services at a fair price, and addressing their claims quickly and effectively. Personal relationships with customers are friendly and caring, respecting their dignity and values. Moreover, they adhere to truthful advertising and commit to open and honest communications, writing business contracts that are fair and easy to understand, never taking advantage of a business relationship.

Relationships with Suppliers

The organization seeks to establish an ethical relationship with suppliers based on fairness, respect and shared benefits. A proper relationship between the organization and suppliers is free from undue pressure, litigation and interest conflicts. Policies, bidding processes and contract management are nondiscriminatory. The relationship implies a mutual commitment based on jointly honoring obligations. On the one hand, the supplier must fulfill the order for products and services as promised in the contract, on schedule, and in the stated amount and quality. On the other, the organization deals with the supplier fairly and pays on time. When meeting these conditions, the relationship benefits both parties: the supplier becomes a *strategic partner*, and the organization gets a dependable supplier that helps the business firm create value and meet the commitments in its mission.

Relationships with the Community

An organization that is an exemplary corporate citizen embraces sustainable practices and actively contributes to the development and flourishing of the communities where it works. It assumes its responsibility in the care and preservation of the environment, complies strictly with the law and pays its fair share of taxes. It integrates into the community by opening communication channels to assess the population's real needs and the social, economic and environmental impact of its actions. It actively participates in areas of interest to the community, facilitates social integration and looks for people's wellbeing. Activities for promoting culture, research and quality of education contribute to a politically, socially and economically sound country. And finally, it encourages employees to adopt a healthy lifestyle and participate in community affairs.

Relationships with Shareholders

Shareholders require professional managers to act responsibly, keep the law and manage for long-term value generation. They also expect to get a fair return for the resources invested and the risk taken. Managers must actively engage with shareholders and provide them with complete and transparent information on businesses and related activities. They must acknowledge that they are the custodian of the resources entrusted to them by a heterogeneous group of shareholders comprising institutional and individual investors.

Therefore, an equitable company is respected and admired by people because it is fair with all stakeholders.

- It offers employees fair compensation.
- It charges reasonable prices to customers and suppliers and transparently relates to them.
- It pays its fair share of taxes to the state.
- It ensures shareholders an appropriate risk-adjusted return for their investment and provides ample information to them.
- It integrates with the community, actively contributing to its progress.
- It also takes the utmost care in its relationship with other companies to ensure the fairness of its actions, avoiding questionable business practices.

The central point is to recognize that management is not only an economic, technical or legal challenge, but primarily a social and ethical challenge.

Sensible leaders contribute to building a better world by participating actively in solving other people's needs in society. Also, they strive to be better human beings in three realms:

- They are faithful to themselves by being aware of the distinct contribution they bring to others. Often being different is difficult, so it requires courage to remain truthful to oneself.
- They develop their talents, being perseverant, and working hard, sometimes for many years.
- They share their learning experiences to inspire followers with a sense of mission.

Creating bonds of trust with all relevant stakeholders is the best way for long-term sustainability and profitability. It is also the best way to make a substantial contribution to the common good and the construction of a Culture of Care.

Note

1 www.weforum.org/agenda/2019/12/davos-manifesto-2020-the-universal-purpose-of-a-company-in-the-fourth-industrial-revolution/

References

Business Roundtable (2019). Business Roundtable redefines the purpose of a corporation to promote "an economy that serves all Americans". Retrieved: www.businessroundtable.org/business-roundtable-redefines-the-purpose-of-a-corporation-to-promote-an-economy-that-serves-all-americans

Hamel, G. (2009). Moonshots for management. *Harvard Business Review*, February, 91–98.

Majluf, N. (2021) A Human Centered Organizational Culture focused on wellbeing, fairness and the common good. In Lepeley, M. T., Morales, O., Essens, P., Beutell, N., and Majluf, N., (eds.). (2021). *Human Centered Organizational Culture: Global Dimensions*. Routledge.

Schwab, K. (2019) What kind of capitalism do we want? *Project Syndicate*, 02 December. Retrieved: www.project-syndicate.org/commentary/stakeholder-capitalism-new-metrics-by-klaus-schwab-2019-11

Senge, P. (2004). *The Fifth Discipline Fieldbook (La quinta disciplina en la práctica)*. Buenos Aires: Granica.

12 Integral Sensible Leadership

Leadership cannot be restricted to the world of work alone. It must consider the whole person, in their various spheres of activity, including home, community and the leader's development as a human being. As Friedman (2008) said: "Leadership isn't just about business. It's about life."

Sensible leaders are *integral leaders* who display human centered behavior in personal and work life. They act in the same way regardless of where or with whom they are. They do not live separate lives. Leading a dissociated life between work and home is harmful. They show appropriate conduct in their corporate world and all areas of their life. As Friedman and Westring (2015) indicate,

> A true leader is one who acts as a leader in all areas of life. I don't want to be an excellent leader at the expense of my family, friends, community, and myself. I want to be a leader in all these domains, acting authentically and being true to my values.

The definition of balance between personal life and work is "the achievement of satisfactory experiences in all domains of life" (Kirchmeyer, 2000). To succeed in this challenge requires allocating personal resources, including energy, time and commitments across all life domains.

The Total Leadership Model (TLM) (Friedman, 2008) provides a guide on how to diagnose the coherence between what individuals would like to do with their life and what they do. In this way, people realize the importance they assign to each one of the four areas of a person's activity: (1) work, career, (2) home and family, (3) community and society, and (4) the person him/herself: mind, body, spirit. This assessment aims at aligning the priorities assigned to each area with the actual time devoted to them. Achieving better integration leads to both a more satisfying life and an enhanced organizational performance.

Such analysis aims at paying a similar amount of attention to all spheres of life to achieve harmony among them and, at the same time, demonstrate authenticity, integrity and creativity. Greater *authenticity* means being yourself in all circumstances, being truthful and making values a way of life and not a simple declaration of principles. Behaving with *integrity* means maintaining and respecting values in all spheres of life. Being *creative* means acting innovatively and experimenting permanently with new, flexible working methods and forms of communication. The powerful combination of greater authenticity, integrity and creativity will ensure achieving both work and personal life goals (Friedman, 2008).

The Life-Work Continuum

A Human Centered Organizational Culture treats life and work as a continuum and focuses on employees' wellbeing. Life is a holistic experience, not a confrontation of separate domains struggling for supremacy. To achieve this integration in life, sensible leaders must pay attention to the negative impact long work hours have on wellbeing. Also, they must implement work-life policies for enabling a proper integration of work and life (Beutell, Kuschel, and Lepeley, 2021).

Sensible leaders face many different demands competing for their time, attention and energy from all areas of personal life and work. The conflict between work and life domains produces an imbalance that Greenhaus and Beutell (1985) formulate as the "scarcity hypothesis". Yet, sensible leaders assume that there is a continuum of work and life. When harmonizing them, there is a transfer of energy, positive experiences and social contacts. This synchrony leads to the "enrichment hypothesis" (Barnett and Hyde, 2001).

The relationship between personal life and career development has evolved from *conflict* to *enrichment*. It reflects a change in leaders' values that "helps participants increase their results by enriching their lives, learning to lead in a different way that integrates work, home, community, and personal development" (Friedman and Westring, 2015). Many studies show a positive relationship between quality of life and other wellbeing indicators (Greenhaus, Collins, and Shaw, 2003; Ochoa, Lepeley, and Essens, 2019).

Leaders adept at handling the demands of multiple roles show a higher level of integration between their work and family lives. Moreover, they present a higher potential for career development than those focused only on their working lives (Lyness and Judiesch, 2008; Beutell, Kuschel, and Lepeley, 2021).

Work-Life Integration Today

Sensible leaders know that work-life integration is now more relevant than ever before. Changes in socio-demographic variables such as parenting, family roles, aging and technology use (including computers, cell phones, internet, the Internet of Things and 5G) continually change people's expectations in terms of life priorities.

Greenblatt (2002) asserts that leaders must pay maximum attention to followers' work-life integration because of the many changes in socio-demographic, technological and political realms. They implement policies and practices to foster wellbeing in the workplace, such as flexible working hours, teleworking and many others.

In the past 20 years, organizations worldwide have recognized the importance of simultaneously meeting the demands of work and personal life. Addressing concerns for work-life integration is now a strategic imperative of sensible leaders because it is the best way to attract, recruit and retain talents. The younger generation considers it essential to integrate personal life and work. To this end, sensible leaders have developed strategies to enlist high-potential employees and manage engagement, morale and stress.

When sensible leaders empower employees with the knowledge and skills to manage multiple roles, they increase engagement and generate greater satisfaction and better performance, leading to long-term organizational sustainability. If employees are happy and the organization is more productive both employees and organization benefit (Friedman and Westring, 2015).

References

Barnett, R. C., and Hyde, J. S. (2001). Women, men, work, and family: an expansionist theory. *American Psychologist*, 56, 781–796.

Beutell, N., Kuschel, K., and Lepeley, M. T. (2021). The work-life continuum. the new Human Centered Organizational Culture. In Lepeley, M.T., Morales, O., Essens, P., Beutell, N., and Majluf, N., (eds.). *Human Centered Organizational Culture: Global Dimensions*. Routledge.

Friedman, S. (2008). *Total Leadership: Be a Better Leader, Have a Richer Life*. Boston, MA: Harvard Business Press.

Friedman, S., and Westring, A. (2015). Empowering individuals to integrate work and life: insights for management development. *Journal of Management Development*, 34, 299–315.

Greenblatt, E. (2002). Work/life balance: wisdom or whining. *Organizational Dynamics*, 31(2), 177–193.

Greenhaus, J. H., and Beutell, N. J. (1985). Sources of conflict between work and family roles. *Academy of Management Review*, 10, 76–88.

Greenhaus, J. H., Collins, K. M., and Shaw, J. D. (2003). The relation between work-family balance and quality of life. *Journal of Vocational Behavior*, 63, 510–531.

Kirchmeyer, C. (2000). Work-life initiatives: greed or benevolence regarding workers' time? In Cooper, C., and Rousseau, D. (Eds.). *Trends in Organizational Behavior: Time in Organizational Behavior*, vol. 7, 79–93.

Lyness, K. S, and Judiesch, M. K. (2008). Can a manager have a life and a career? International and multisource perspectives on work-life balance and career advancement potential. *Journal of Applied Psychology*, 93(4), 789–805.

Ochoa, P., Lepeley, M. T., and Essens, P. (2019). *Wellbeing for Sustainability in the Global Workplace*. Routledge.

13 The Sensible Leader is an Ethical Leader

The sensible, human centered, insightful and prudent leader is an *ethical leader* who inspires followers to engage enthusiastically in the defined organization's mission. They lead by example, living the values they cherish in three realms: their relationship with followers, the subtle management of power and political processes in the organization, and the relations with stakeholders.

An ethical leader perceives the ethical dilemmas present in the decisions they confront. It is not an easy task because people are limited and face decisions that are often hard to deal with. Even well-meant people who have noble feelings and want to do good do not always succeed. It is not surprising. Humans are limited beings, living in an imperfect world, with flawed organizations and companies and an insufficient government. It is necessary to recognize these huge limitations and accept the frailty of institutions. This does not imply settling for less and giving up with a sense of fatalism, but striving to improve as much as possible and, simultaneously, being patient with mistakes, learning from them and preventing them from happening again.

Moreover, to develop, follow and transmit ethical principles, sensible leaders must deal with daily disruptions in the global VUCA environment. And although social, economic, cultural, demographic and technological changes have brought wellbeing in the form of goods and services for a better life, they also cause frustration because of unfulfilled expectations. Additionally, they generate anger due to the perception of abuses and inequality. Understanding the underlying forces of society is a complex matter. Solutions are complicated, demanding and involve unperceived or undiscovered ethical dilemmas. Just appreciating the situation and comprehending the moral quandaries is an essential quality of a sensible leader.

Professor Joseph Badaracco's comment on the definition of leaders idealized as gifted individuals, highlighting their shortcomings and the difficulties of their task, states that "leadership is a struggle by flawed human beings to make some important human values real and effective, in the world as it is".[1]

Ethical leaders have developed the ability to perceive and assess the difficulties and dilemmas that arise in a complicated situation, as when confronting conflicting interests and visions of different social actors. Also, they must prepare to face them because ethical dilemmas are difficult choices. Whatever the preferred alternative, there is a cost that they would rather avoid. For instance, when considering a worthwhile project for the country that generates harm for a local community: if the project is approved, the local community is worse off; if it is not supported, society loses. There is no win-win situation. It is an instance of the *Principle of Double Effect*, according to which there is a good to be obtained, but there is no way to avoid damaging some people. Even if there is no intention to generate damage, it cannot be avoided. That explains the lucid explanation of Professor Joseph Badaracco from Harvard when stating that ethical decisions are not about choosing between right and wrong, but between right and right, instead.

Ethical leadership needs to be within a strict ethical framework. Firstly, because it is the right thing to do, but also because of the visibility of leaders that makes them role models to follow. And the behavior of leaders is not always the most appropriate. Their weaknesses as human beings mean that they are often unable to live up to the ethical demands of their position. It has historically been a cause of great pain in organizations and is undoubtedly a dire circumstance. And today, this difficulty is even more severe because with the emergence of sharp journalism and social networks that expand the news at high speed and without limitations, inadequate behavior profoundly impacts the entire organization. Instead of getting the support and enthusiasm of followers, this surprises them, cools their interest and disengages them.

More than ever, leadership in our time demands ethical guidance based on values and oriented to service to others. To avoid losing the moral compass in a changing environment, ethical leaders must cultivate their moral reasoning and exercise *value-based leadership* and *service-oriented leadership*.

Preparing to Be a Leader: Cultivating Moral Reasoning

Ethical decisions require a systematic analysis. Leaders need to gather information, consult experts, make analyses, determine the pros and cons and consider the benefits and costs in the different decision alternatives. But this is not enough. Ethical dilemmas require another form of analysis. An objective, rigorous and scientific evaluation of alternative options illuminates decisions, but they are ultimately decisions in conscience. The choice is between two good alternatives that bring unwanted harmful side effects (the *Principle of Double Effect*).

So, regardless of the effort made to collect information, conduct in-depth analyses or consult respectable and wise people, the ethical dilemma won't go away.

Being sensitive to the difficulty of deciding in these situations produces uneasiness because the best course of action is not apparent. When confronting ethical dilemmas, there is no correct answer, and regardless of the decision, some damage neither wanted nor sought will result.

Experiencing this anxiety level requires leaders to act prudently and cultivate tolerance for ambiguity; otherwise, they cannot overcome the personal stress of living through these situations. Their solitude and agony are unavoidable and bring them discomfort because, ultimately, the impact of ethical decisions is a concern that overwhelms them.

Without a doubt, to move more confidently when confronting an ethical decision, leaders must prepare themselves with some methodology to strengthen their moral reasoning. Two primary arguments are behind the need for this preparation (Sucher, 2007). First, leaders face challenges brought about by changes in the organizational context. They must make difficult decisions affecting different groups of people positively or negatively. In these circumstances, selecting a course of action, whatever it may be, implies compromises between the short- and long-term *goods* and *burdens* imposed on these different groups. Second, various internal and external groups, with distinct personal views, populate organizations, resulting in an ever-widening range of discrepancies and a high level of tension between them. In a global world, these differences are still more profound.

Leaders should permanently deepen and refine the ethical principles that guide their actions and do their best to form their conscience and cultivate a virtuous behavior. This behavior does not make them a saint, but a person who understands the depth of their responsibilities and strives to do their best.

Two fundamental ethical principles are central in evaluating the impact of ethical decisions: "the primacy of the human being by their dignity and freedom" and "the common good".[2]

Value-based Leadership

Ethical leaders pursue value-based management (Majluf and Navarrete, 2011) being role models of personal conduct. Their actions and decisions contribute to institutionalizing an organization's ethical culture. They help promote ethical principles and live the values underlying these principles, beyond solely well-meaning declarations, with actions leading to enhanced wellbeing and the minimization of ethical conflicts in the organization.

Ethical leaders seek to balance multiple values to manage the Human Centered organization, including fairness, trust, transparency, responsibility and honesty. But beyond promoting a set of values, value-based leadership rests on self-control supported by establishing institutions, procedures and rules that allow for self-regulation. Also, it rests on the creation of a *culture of integrity* that provides an ethical framework.

A culture of integrity emphasizes the organization's social role and places the human being at the center of decision making. It is a matter of raising awareness on the impact that any decision has over followers and stakeholders, including the community. The challenge is to address the decision-making process with an ethical perspective. The leaders' style and conduct, jointly with open communication policies and systems of recognition, promotion and performance assessment, shape the culture of integrity and encourage ethical behavior. It is the only way to ensure that ethical criteria and not economic or other criteria shape the pattern of an organization's actions.

Organizations directed by ethical leaders place ethical values at the center and become institutions open to the community and committed to meet the needs and demands of their constituencies. They are unequivocally committed to sustainable national development and global progress.

Ethical organizations strive for social diversity, inclusion and the wellbeing of people. They participate actively in promoting culture, improving education quality (Lepeley, 2019a), supporting research, alleviating poverty and fostering sustainable development (Lepeley, 2019b). They encourage their employees' participation in community affairs and promote a healthy style in both life and work. In short, they are organizations integrated into society trying to be a *good citizen*, contributing to a politically, socially, environmentally and economically healthy environment in the country, and working for the common good. It is a form of leadership centered on the wellbeing of people, inside and outside the organization.

Finally, ethical leaders are custodians of the legacy that shapes culture and traditions treasured by society. Leaders' mettle appears when they must choose between their interests and the values of which they are custodians and do not hesitate to postpone their wellbeing. This type of leadership is particularly valid in the context of political leaders, who are not just:

> the administrators of government bureaus. They are more than the writers of laws. They are the custodians of a nation's ideals, of the beliefs it cherishes, of its permanent hopes, of the faith which makes a nation out of a mere aggregation of individuals.
>
> Walter Lippmann, quoted in McKinney (2000)

Being a custodian is a way of being, of seeing the world, of living life. And it is also a great responsibility that requires knowing how to identify those things, values and traditions cherished by other people; what is right, ethical and lasting for those we serve.

Service-oriented Leadership

"The most pressing and unavoidable question is, what are you doing for others?" This compelling call was Martin Luther King's admonition in his well-known "Strength to Love" speech of 1963.[3] Assuming responsibility for followers' wellbeing is a personal project that gives meaning to leaders' lives. A deep-seated need to rise above conventional norms and customs and embrace a culture of service that transforms leaders into servants and coaches is at the heart of human nature. To achieve that, they modify organizational structures and systems and encourage cooperative behavior and participation in decision-making to build a culture of service and trust (Covey, 2019).

The definitive test of their intentions is to ask:

- Whether those they serve are growing as human beings and are wiser, freer, more autonomous, healthier
- Whether the less privileged will benefit in any way or, at the very least, not suffer any additional detriment
- Whether they have increased their chances of becoming service-oriented leaders themselves
- Or whether the world is different (and better) because of the things they've done (Bordas, 2015)

This form of leadership has deep ethical roots revealed in the concern for people's wellbeing, the efforts to enhance the personal growth of followers and the energy displayed in the improvement of institutions. It is the central concern of the extensive "servant leadership" literature (Greenleaf, 1977, 2002). The two fundamental questions of service-oriented leadership are: Whom do you serve? And What is your purpose?

This form of leadership is practiced by those giving precedence to serving others, promoting a sense of community, providing ample space for participation in decision-making, and prioritizing the needs of employees, customers and the community. These leaders feel a deep urge to serve people, attending to their most essential needs and aspirations. Leadership is a vocation of service for the benefit of people over and above personal interests. They tirelessly pursue the common good.

This is not always the case. Many times, leaders have different or opposite purposes to the noble objective of serving others. Maidique (2011) identifies six different types of leaders. Level-VI, which he calls "Transcendent Leader", focuses on the common good, and their daily interest is to make the world a better place. The other levels are:

Level V or "Builders" focus on creating an enduring institution and caring for their development and progress. They are oriented to the long term and do not fall into the trap of short-term benefits. Their vision of the future, energy, enthusiasm and integrity are contagious.

Level IV leaders are achievement-oriented. They effectively accomplish what their superiors (their boss, the board of directors, the law) have defined for them, no questions asked.

The other three levels correspond to individuals who can hardly be called leaders. Level III leaders change with the prevailing winds. Level II leaders show opportunistic behavior with no regard for their friends, family, society or the institution they are supposed to serve. They merely seek their benefit. And level I leaders are sociopaths who serve neither themselves nor their surroundings.

The service-oriented leader in this book is Level-VI. These leaders go beyond their organization's boundaries to serve the community without overlooking their institution's progress.

The motivation in service-oriented leaders comes mainly from the sense of transcendence (meaning) of the task, its impact on society and its contribution to creating a better world. It is not only from extrinsic (monetary) or intrinsic (psychological) rewards. Even though people expect economic benefits for their work, they are also willing to work without expecting anything in return. It isn't easy to draw the line between monetary-driven behavior and pure generosity, but the fairness of compensation plays an important role. When people feel that their payment is fair, they are more engaged and are willing to exercise their generosity. On the contrary, when the feeling is of unfairness, transcendent motivation will dwindle. Undoubtedly, motivation is affected by economic remuneration, but it is wrong to assume that a higher payment is always better for the organization or the individual's satisfaction. Money is not essential in motivating people unless they are in a borderline survival condition (Chomali and Majluf, 2008; Faúndez, 2006; Pérez-López, 1991; Chinchilla-Albiol and Donaldo, 2011; Chamorro-Premuzic, 2013).

Surprisingly, traditional leadership theories are centered on the leader's person and say so little of the impact of their actions and decisions on society at large. They ignore that one of the most potent forms of self-fulfillment is serving others. It is an important reason to assert that leadership in our time has an ethical dimension that is impossible to ignore.

Choosing service over self-interest (McKinney, 2000) is an act of detachment for the benefit of others. It is a way of life that gives special attention to other people's interests, particularly followers. It is not the perks that leaders can achieve in their position that are important to service-oriented leaders.

Authentic leadership has always been an altruistic action that focuses on others' needs and thinks over what is best for the common good. Leadership is virtuous only if the community's wellbeing is above all other considerations, even in the most straightforward and ordinary daily life situations, like the exercise of leadership in relationships with friends and family. Sensible, human centered leaders are all called to become custodians of what is enduring and valuable to those they serve.

Notes

1 Quoted in Snyder (2013).
2 Based on the Compendium of Social Doctrine of the Catholic Church, Chapter 4. Revised in: www.vatican.va/roman_curia/pontifical_councils/ justpeace/documents/rc_pc_justpeace_doc_20060526_compendio-dott-soc_ sp.html
3

Light has come into the world, and every man must decide whether he will walk in the light of creative altruism or the darkness of destructive selfishness. This is the judgment. Life's most persistent and urgent question is, 'What are you doing for others?'.

Martin Luther King, Jr., Strength to Love, 1963

References

Bordas, J. (2015). Pluralistic reflections on servant-leadership, cited in Ferch, S., Spears, L., McFarland, M., and Carey, M. (eds.) *Conversations on Servant-Leadership: Insights on Human Courage in Life and Work*. Albany, NY: State University of New York Press.
Chamorro-Premuzic, T. (2013) Does money really affect motivation? A review of the research, *Harvard Business Review*, April 13.
Chinchilla-Albiol, M. N., and Cruz-Rivas, H. D. (2011). A new approach to diversity and organizational paradigms (Diversidad y paradigmas de empresa: un nuevo enfoque). *Revista empresa y humanismo*, 14(1), 47–79.
Chomali, F., and Majluf, N. (2008). *Business Ethics and Social Responsibility (Ética y responsabilidad social en la empresa)*. Santiago, Chile: El Mercurio-Aguilar.
Covey, S. (2019). How the best leaders build trust. Retrieved www.leadershipnow. com/CoveyOnTrust.html
Faúndez, D. (2006). *Ethical leadership: the impact on subordinates (Liderazgo con sentido ético: impacto en los subordinados)*. Tesis para optar al Grado de Magíster en Ciencias de la Ingeniería, Pontificia Universidad Católica de Chile.
Greenleaf, R. K. (1977, 2002). *Servant Leadership: A Journey into the Nature of Legitimate Power and Greatness*, 25th Anniversary Edition, Mahwah, NJ: Paulist Press.
Lepeley, M. T. (2019a). *EDUQUALITY. Human Centered Quality Management in Education. A Model for Assessment, Deployment and Sustainability*. Charlotte, NC: Information Age Publishing.
Lepeley, M. T. (2019b). *EDUCONOMY. Unleashing Wellbeing and Human Centered Sustainable Development*. Charlotte, NC: Information Age Publishing.
Maidique, M. (2011). Are you a level-six leader? *Research and Ideas: Harvard Business School Working Knowledge*, July 6. Retrieved: https://business.fiu. edu/pdf/PrintJan2012/z%20level-six-leader.pdf
Majluf, N., and Navarrete, C. (2011). A two-component compliance and ethics program model an empirical application to Chilean corporations. *Journal of Business Ethics*, 100, 567–579. Retrieved: https://doi.org/10.1007/ s10551-010-0696-6

McKinney, M. (2000). The Focus of Leadership: Choosing Service Over Self-Interest, LeadershipNow.com. Retrieved www.leadershipnow.com/service.html

Pérez-López, J. A. (1991), *Theory of Human Action in Organizations (Teoría de la Acción Humana en las Organizaciones)*. Madrid: Rialp.

Snyder, S. (2013). *Leadership and the Art of Struggle*. San Francisco, CA: Berrett-Koehler Publishers.

Sucher, S. (2007). Lessons from the classroom: teaching the moral leader. *Harvard Business School Working Knowledge*, November 19.

Index

Made in the USA
Middletown, DE
11 April 2023

28631847R00082